D1487771

O COME EMMANUEL

W. J. Marshall

O Come Emmanuel

SCRIPTURE VERSES
FOR ADVENT WORSHIP

MOREHOUSE PUBLISHING
Harrisburg, PA

First published in Ireland in 1993 by The Columba Press and APCK

First U.S. Edition published in 1994 by

Morehouse Publishing
P.O. Box 1321
Harrisburg, PA 17105

The blessing on page 41 is used by kind permission of the Indian Society for Promoting Christian Knowledge, Delhi.

Library of Congress Cataloging-in-Publication Data
Marshall, W. J., Ph.D.
   O come Emmanuel : a study of the Advent antiphons / W. J. Marshall.
—1st U.S. ed.
      p.   cm.
   Originally published: Ireland: Columba Press and APCK, 1993.
   ISBN 0-8192-1629-1 (pbk.)
   1. Advent.   2. O antiphons.   3. Antiphons (Music)—Texts—History
and criticism.   4. Advent hymns—Texts—History and criticism.
5. Jesus Christ—Name.   I. Title.
BV40.M37   1994   94-12745
264'.1—dc20   CIP

Printed in the United States of America

Contents

Acknowledgements

Through the generosity of my former parish, Rathmichael, I was able to take study leave at St Deiniol's Library, Hawarden, where I wrote most of this book. In gratitude I dedicate it to the people of Rathmichael. I also thank Dr Peter Jagger and the staff of St Deiniol's for their encouragement and assistance. I am indebted to Mrs Caroline Kennedy who typed much of the book and I thank my wife Margaret for help with the proof-reading and encouragement generally.

William Marshall
May 1993

Introduction

The form in which the Advent antiphons are known to most people is the hymn 'O come, O come, Emmanuel', a nineteenth century translation by J. M. Neale of a thirteenth century Latin hymn by an unknown author. The medieval hymn was based on five of the seven antiphons appointed to be sung before and after the *Magnificat* at Vespers on the days before Christmas Eve. In addition, the hymn had a freshly composed chorus which is reproduced in the English version.

Antiphons are verses repeated before and after a psalm or canticle to emphasise a particular thought. The service of Compline, for example, gives the *Nunc Dimittis* the antiphon:

> Save us, O Lord, while waking, and guard us while sleeping, that while we are awake we may watch with Christ, and when we sleep we may rest in peace.

This antiphon shows the meaning of the *Nunc Dimittis* for ordinary Christians as they recite it in their evening prayers. Originally it was Simeon's glad prayer of self-committal to God when he saw the infant Christ towards the end of his days. We use it to express a similar trust in God at evening time as we ask him to guard our waking and our sleeping.

The Advent antiphons similarly interpret the *Magnificat* for the period just before Christmas. According to St Luke's account, Mary uttered the *Magnificat* when she visited her kinswoman Elizabeth after the angel had announced to her that she was to be the mother of our Lord. It is a joyful outburst of praise to God for the incredible honour he has done her in choosing her to give birth to the Saviour. It is full of thankful wonder at the great salvation God has given to Israel in fulfilment of his promise. As a song about the coming of the Saviour, the *Magnificat* is particularly suited to the Advent season and needs no great transposition to proclaim the Advent message, but the antiphons emphasise and fill out that message by invoking God and Christ under the titles of Wisdom, Adonai, Emmanuel and so on.

In the development of the Church's daily round of worship, antiphons for psalms and canticles were appointed for special seasons and ordinary times in ever-increasing complexity. But no other set of antiphons acquired the position of those for the latter part of Advent which became known as the Great 'O's. We can speculate about why they should have captured the imagination of Christians above all others. They have a distinctive form, each beginning with a title of God, or Jesus, preceded by the longing cry 'O'. They each contain the prayer 'come' followed by 'and ...' with different verbs: teach, deliver, bring out, enlighten, save. The titles are archetypal words – key, light, root – which evoke deep feelings and thoughts in universal human experience. The Latin hymn which the antiphons inspired, and its English translation in the nineteenth century, greatly enhanced their appeal and made them much more widely known, but they must have had some special quality to occasion the hymn in the first place.

The antiphons may be used in the traditional way with the *Magnificat*, but they also have a meaning in their own right and their use as a hymn or litany will probably appeal more to Christians today.

As originally composed, the antiphons consist almost entirely of the words of Scripture in St Jerome's Latin version known as the Vulgate. They were introduced to the daily worship of the Western Church before the ninth century. In the standard form there are seven antiphons, which will be the subject of this study, but some service books have eight and the Sarum Breviary has nine. Evidently the first one, *O Sapientia*, was used on 16 December and when the usual pattern was followed, 21 December, St Thomas' Day, was omitted from the sequence. Some time after the Reformation, the seven antiphons began on 17 December and continued without a break until the day before Christmas Eve.

The Reformation in England had as one of its aims to restore the Church's public worship to the 'godly and decent order of the ancient Fathers' (Preface to the 1549 Prayer Book). Accordingly Thomas Cranmer, the reforming Archbishop of Canterbury, translated the Latin services into English in a much reduced and simplified form, which included the systematic reading of the Bible throughout the year. 'For this cause,' he wrote, 'be cut off Anthems [antiphons], Responds, Invitatories, and such like things as did break the continual course of the reading of the Scripture' (*ibid*). Hence the Advent antiphons disappeared from Anglican worship until they were revived, in Neale's translation of the hymn based on them, in the nineteenth century. The only trace left was in the Calendar, where *O Sapientia* is listed as a black letter holy day in the *Book of Common Prayer* from 1604.

Everyone would agree that the complexity of the service books in the late Middle Ages greatly needed revision, particularly since Cranmer's rather idealistic aim was to encourage lay people to join in the Church's Morning and Evening Prayer daily. But inevitably something of value in the old order was lost and the seven Advent antiphons are a notable example. They are entirely scriptural, their use has no taint of superstition attached to them, and they do not hinder 'the continual course of the reading of the Scripture'.

The Second Vatican Council had a number of aims similar to those of the Reformation, including that of enabling the whole people of God to join actively in worship. After the Council, the liturgy of the Mass and the Divine Office (daily services) was revised and translated into the vernaculars of the world-wide Church. An English version of the Divine Office was published in 1976 under the title *Morning and Evening Prayer*. It reduced the seven daily services to three (Compline was retained as a late evening office) and simplified them, with the deliberate intention of encouraging their use by lay people as well as those clergy and religious not required by their rule to say the full Divine Office. Evening Prayer contains the seven Advent antiphons in modern English, with the rubric that they are to be recited before and after the *Magnificat*, 17-23 December.

Neale's hymn is the best known of a number, based on the antiphons, which appeared in the nineteenth century and is included in the hymn books of nearly all denominations today. The *English Hymnal* (1906) has a different translation by T. A. Lacey. There were also a number of prose versions, one of which is given in the *English Hymnal*. Some modern Anglican prayer books have restored the antiphons for use before and after the Magnificat from 16 December, South Africa (1954) and India (1960). The Canadian *Book of Alternative Services* (1985) gives them in a modern language version as a litany for use in Advent with the response, 'Lord Jesus, come soon.' The Church of England published, in 1991, a supplementary book for Advent, Christmas and Epiphany entitled *Promise of his Glory* which contains an Advent service built round the Great 'O's' in both verse and prose forms. It also makes them into a litany with the response, 'Maranatha. Come, Lord Jesus.'

The version we shall use is that in the *English Hymnal* but omitting an eighth antiphon, *O Virgo Virginum*, found there. The archaic language of that version is a quite literal translation of the Latin and is useful for tracing the biblical references. However, modern language versions will be referred to when they bring out some special point. The hymn which Neale and others translated only deals with five of the seven antiphons, leaving out *O Sapientia* and *O Rex Gentium*. However, a recent edition of the *English Hymnal* has added two verses based on the missing antiphons, presumably newly composed. At the head of each chapter, I have given the text of the antiphon and the corresponding verse from Neale's hymn. For *O Sapientia* and *O Rex Gentium*, I have used the hymn verses from the *English Hymnal*. Where there is a development of thought in the hymn this will be noted.

10

Since the antiphons are largely words of Scripture, the relevant Bible verses are also given at the beginning of each chapter. They are usually quoted in the Revised Standard Version, except occasionally in the Authorised Version where it is closer to the antiphon. Since those who originally compiled the antiphons used the Vulgate, the reason for a particular word or turn of phrase can often be found by looking up the verse in that version. I have given the Latin texts of the antiphons and of the hymn in the appendices.

Father Geoffrey Preston O.P. has discussed each of the Advent antiphons in his book on the Christian year, *Hallowing the Time* (D.L.T. London 1980). I have been greatly helped by his insights and knowledge. My own approach is different from his in that it is based on the biblical texts which make up the antiphons and others connected with them. I look at them in their original contexts, their meaning in the antiphons and their inter-relations. It is my hope that this study may uncover something of the riches to be found in the Advent antiphons and may aid our devotion to the Christ who came, who comes and who is to come.

CHAPTER 1

Our Hearts' Desire

The Advent antiphons are known as 'the great "O"s', from the initial 'O' of each one, which conveys our longing for the coming of the Lord. The longings of the human heart are part of the glory of humanity. Why do people climb Everest, explore potholes, cross the Antarctic on foot or the Atlantic in a rowing boat, build cathedrals like Chartres or tombs like the Taj Mahal, write and read poetry, compose and listen to symphonies? We discover in ourselves 'high instincts before which our mortal nature did tremble like a guilty thing surprised.' There is a yearning for the transcendent, even among moderns who have done so much to make the world a comfortable place to live in.

It is the conviction, not only of Christians but of all who believe in a personal God, that this longing is implanted in us by God and can only be satisfied by him. All our desires are, in one form or another, a desire for God. Sometimes desires conflict with one another and with our desire for God, but when purified and graded according to their true value, they will be seen as a longing for God in his manifold being and activity. Love for things and for other human beings reaches fulfilment in subordination to love of God.

The Bible, especially the Psalms, is full of man's longing for God, often under the figures of hunger and thirst which were physically familiar to the ancient inhabitants of the near East in a way modern western readers cannot appreciate. 'O God, thou art my God, early will I seek thee, my soul thirsteth for thee, my flesh longeth for thee in a dry and thirsty land where no water is' (Ps 63:1 *A.V.*).

The Jewish people longed for the coming of a Messiah who would restore their country to the greatness it enjoyed in the days of King David. There were crude, nationalistic elements in this aspiration, represented in Christ's time by the Zealot party whose futile uprising resulted in the destruction of Jerusalem by the Romans in AD 70. Yet it would be wrong to think that genuine longing for a Messiah must be purely spiritual. The Jews suffered invasion after invasion, deportation after deportation, and they earnestly prayed that God would come to them in power, bring them back to their own land, free them from foreign rule and restore their national dignity under the sovereignty of God. The city and temple of Jerusalem was the focus of their longings. 'Pray for the peace of Jerusalem! "May they prosper who love you! Peace be within your walls, and security within your towers!"' (Ps 122: 6, 7). This sentiment is found in many psalms: God's presence and the holy city are not the same thing but they are closely associated. The people's longing for God is embodied in the temple on mount Zion: 'This is my dwelling place for ever; here will I dwell for I have desired it' (Ps 132: 14). In the messianic longings of the Jews, the material and the spiritual are blended in a living whole.

The longings which the antiphons express are answered in their associated canticle, the *Magnificat*, which sees the promises of God fulfilled both in material and spiritual terms. The Blessed Virgin in this song praises God that 'he has come to the help of his servant Israel' (Lk 1:54) in fulfilment of his promise which includes the overthrow of the mighty and the raising up of the lowly, the feeding of the hungry and the rejection of the rich. The other canticle relating to Christ's coming, the *Benedictus*, the song of John the Baptist's father, Zechariah, is even more explicit in giving a political dimension to the freedom Christ brings. God 'has raised up for us a mighty saviour' (Lk 1:69). He had promised that he would 'set us free from the hands of our enemies, free to worship him without fear; holy and righteous in his sight all the days of our life' (vv. 74, 75. Quotations from the canticles are in the ICET version).

Zechariah and the Virgin Mary are thoroughly Jewish in the way they see the coming of the Messiah. He is the one who brings freedom to his people in the fullest sense. Jesus Christ fulfilled, corrected and enlarged the Jewish concept of the Messiah, in particular by teaching that he must suffer. However, the full dimensions of the freedom Christ brings must not be reduced in reaction to the excessively political ideas of Jesus' contemporaries. Christ inaugurated God's kingdom on earth and that means bringing everything – all aspects of human life and indeed all creation – under God's rule. His coming is good news to the poor, release to the captives, sight to the blind and liberty to the oppressed (Lk 4: 18, quoting Is 61:1) as well as bringing forgiveness of sins. Liberation theology may be one-sided, but it has alerted us to aspects of the good news of Christ which have been neglected in the past.

We speak disparagingly of 'cupboard love' in pets and children, but their frank enjoyment of the good things they receive from parents and owners shows a genuine, uncomplicated love without any attempt to analyse its constituent elements. A child-like love which looks for presents may be more pleasing to God than one which is wholly disinterested and high-minded. Other desires can be rivals to our desires for God, but they can also be included in that desire. Given a subordinate place, they can receive full satisfaction in God's infinite bounty. 'Seek first God's kingdom and his righteousness and all these things shall be yours as well' (Mt 6: 33).

The deepest longings of our hearts find their satisfaction in the coming of Christ. Both Advent and Christmas celebrate that coming. Christmas relates primarily to the historic event of his birth; Advent draws attention to the wider aspects of his coming. The Christ who was born on earth promised his disciples that he would come again. 'When I go and prepare a place for you, I will come again and take you to myself, that where I am you may be also' (Jn 14: 3). This 'coming again' refers to the indescribable revelation of Christ in glory which brings this age to a close, but not exclusively so. There are many intimations, anticipations, of that great event in the present age when Christ continually comes. He came to his disciples when he appeared to them after his resurrect- ion and in the coming of the Holy Spirit at Pentecost. He comes when two or three gather in his name and when they celebrate the Eucharist showing forth his death 'till he come.' St Paul can speak of Christians as now risen and seated with Christ in the heavenly places (Eph 2: 6), a foretaste of their reigning with him in glory. Christ comes to the world in the hungry, naked, prisoner and stranger needing our help. The Christian lives between the times of Christ's coming to earth as a human being and his final coming in glory. This in-between time is not one of absence but of contin- ual coming. It is only because Christ is present with us now that we long and pray for his fuller manifestation. Pascal imagines God saying to the human seeker, 'You would not be seeking me if you had not already found me' (*Pensées* No. 554). Similarly, the presence of Christ in sacrament, prayer and love of our neighbour, makes us eager for his coming in glory. The antiphons address Christ by such titles as wisdom, Lord and Emmanuel, asking him to come and deliver us, and the people's response in the Canadian Prayer Book is, 'Lord Jesus, come soon.'

'Maranatha,' 'Come O Lord,' was a prayer constantly on the lips of the early Christians, so much so that it retained its Aramaic form among Greek speakers. They saw their earthly lives as transitory and limited and knew they should be always ready for the com- ing of their Lord. Sometimes they spent whole nights in prayer in the spirit of Christ's words, 'Blessed are those servants, whom the Lord when he cometh shall find watching' (Lk 12: 37 *AV*). They expected the return of Jesus in glory during their own lifetime and had no conception of centuries of history after them. Events proved them wrong on that point, but not in their outlook and vision of human life in a precarious world lit up by the presence of Christ and the promise of his more glorious appearing. They could rejoice because 'The Lord is at hand' (Phil 4: 4,5). Even while waiting and longing for the return of their Lord they could appreciate any 'excellence', anything that is true, pure and lovely (*ibid* v.8) in this passing scene, without setting their hearts on the world. In the passage referred to, St Paul uses terms current among Greek moralists, especially the Stoics, such as 'excellence', *areté*, a key term in Stoic ethics. Supreme devotion to Christ should not make us despise human culture but rather value it as coming from God.

The Advent antiphons use words mainly from the Old Testament to refer to the coming of Christ. Hence they are chiefly about his first coming as a man to earth, the Christmas theme. They look ahead to his coming in terms of longing for the Messiah. In the days before Christmas, it is helpful to try and enter the thoughts and expectations of devout Jews waiting for the Messiah, like the aged Simeon and the eighty-year-old Anna, who were 'looking for the consolation of Israel' (Lk 2:25). Yet the antiphons need not be taken exclusively in connection with Christ's birth on earth. They are very much a cry for Christ's coming into the turmoil of modern life, 'Come and teach us', 'Come and deliver us', 'Enlighten him that sitteth in darkness', and they reach out to his final and glorious appearing, 'Tarry not', 'Come and save mankind'. In the chorus of the Latin hymn based on the antiphons, and its English version, there is an interesting variation. The Latin reads '… *Emmanuel nascetur pro te, Israel'*, literally 'Emmanuel shall be born for thee, Israel'. The English rendering is 'Emmanuel shall come to thee… ' No doubt the variation is due to need for rhythm in the English, but the result is a happy extension of the meaning to include all aspects of Christ's coming.

Each of the antiphons contains the words 'O' and 'Come', expressive of longing, pleading, heart-felt desire. In them we beg God to be with us and save us. Yet, in many cases, they are based on words in the Bible which promise exactly that, or even state that God has already come and delivered us. The petition 'Come and redeem us, tarry not' is based on God's promise 'my salvation will not tarry' (Is 46:13). 'Come and enlighten him that sitteth in darkness and the shadow of death' echoes the Christmas reading 'they that dwell in the land of the shadow of death, upon them hath the light shined (Is. 9:2 *AV*). Why should we ask for what God already wills to give us? But that, and that alone, is precisely what we should ask for. The object of prayer is not to change God's will but to conform our wills to his. Why, then, do we need to ask him for anything? Why not just submit to his will? Simply pray 'Thy will be done'? Here we face the problem of petitionary prayer about which millions of words must have been written. Part of the difficulty, at least, springs from too abstract a view of human life and our relationship with God. It has often been said that there are no atheists in a ship about to perish at sea. The urge to beg God to come to our aid in cases like that is so strong, so natural and instinctive, that even a totally secular upbringing can hardly stifle it. Far from being ashamed of such an attitude, Christ taught us that it is exactly how God wishes us to look on him, as a father who cares for his children and is always eager to listen when they ask him. God could give us good things without our asking him and he often does. But when we receive gifts from God in answer to prayer, a child-father relationship of loving trust is established and strengthened. There are some things even God can't do for us unless we want him to. As free human beings we can only receive that friendship and communion with him, which is his highest gift, if we willingly ask for and accept it. St Augustine said, 'God does not ask us to tell him about our needs in order to learn about them, but in order that we may be made capable of receiving his gifts' (quoted in Kenneth Stevenson, *Accept this Offering*, SPCK 1989, p. 35). The prayer of the antiphons, 'Come and deliver us', is made with the confidence expressed in the *Magnificat*, 'He has come to the help of his servant Israel.' It is an entirely appropriate prayer to the God who is more ready to hear than we to pray, and wont to give more than either we desire or deserve. It helps us receive his gifts.

The longing for God expressed in the antiphons is the pale, human shadow of God's longing for us. God does not need us; he is perfect and complete without us, so to speak of his longing for us can be misleading. The traditional Christian teaching is that God's creation of the universe, including the human race, is an act of pure gift-love. Irenaeus writes, 'It was not because God needed man that he first formed Adam, he was simply looking for recipients who might receive his benefits' (*Against Heresies*, Book 4, 13). Hence when we speak of God's longing for us, we have to remember that it is not like a thirsty man's longing for a drink, or even a mother's longing for the child on whom she pours out her love. The first is a straightforward need, the second a more subtle kind of need – to be needed, to give. God is all-sufficient, and that makes his love for us all the more wonderful because it is completely gratuitous. Yet to speak of God's love for us as a 'longing', with all the word's human limitations, is closer to the truth than Aristotle's cold and abstract concept of God as the 'unmoved Mover', or Spinoza's austere dictum, 'He who loves God should not expect that God should love him in return.' While there are dangers in using human terms to describe God, the dangers in avoiding them totally are even greater. The biblical authors do not hesitate to ascribe human emotions to God in order to convey the warmth and passion of his love. Hosea hears God pleading with Israel, 'How can I give you up, O Ephraim! How can I hand you over, O Israel! ... My heart recoils within me, my compassion grows warm and tender' (Hos 11:9). Jesus reveals to us that quality in God of which mother-love is the closest earthly example. 'O Jerusalem, Jerusalem, killing the prophets and stoning those who are sent to you! How often would I have gathered you together as a hen gathers her brood under her wings, and you would not!' (Lk 13:34).

God longs for us, longs for our love and devotion, longs to give us the cup of joy which is communion with him, longs to share with us the vision of eternal beauty, truth and goodness. God's longing creates in us a human, creaturely longing for his gifts and above all for himself. The Advent antiphons articulate that longing under different figures – Wisdom, Root of Jesse, Key of David, Emmanuel – and give us the words in which to pour out, though we may not recognise it, the deepest desire of our hearts. Thomas Merton, who entered the Trappist monastery of Gethsemani, Kentucky, in the Advent of 1941, found that his renunciation of the world, echoed by the winter bareness of the land, heightened the sense of longing which ran through the Advent liturgy. 'Everything that the Church gives you to sing, every prayer that you say in and with Christ in his Mystical Body, is a cry of ardent desire for grace, for help, for the coming of the Messiah, the Redeemer' (Thomas Merton, *The Seven Storey Mountain*, Sheldon Press, 1975, p. 379). 'Everyday, from now on, the office would ring with the deep impassioned cries of the old prophets calling out to God to send the Redeemer. *Veni, Domine, noli tardare ...*' (*ibid* p. 380). The majority of Christians, who find their vocation in a no less demanding life in the world, can also use the Advent antiphons to bring to the surface their deep-rooted longing for God.

CHAPTER 2

O Wisdom

O Sapientia. O Wisdom, which camest out of the mouth of the Most High, and reachest from one end to the other, mightily and sweetly ordering all things: Come and teach us the way of prudence.

O come, thou Wisdom from on High!
Who madest all in earth and sky,
Creating man from dust and clay:
To us reveal salvation's way.

I [wisdom] came forth from the mouth of the Most High (Sir 24:3).

She [wisdom] reaches mightily from one end of the earth to the other, and she orders all things well (Wis 8:1).

The best known building in Istanbul is the church of Santa Sophia, or Hagia Sophia, 'Holy Wisdom', built by the Emperor Justinian in the sixth century AD, converted into a mosque by the Turks in 1452, and now a museum in modern secular Turkey. For most of its existence, it was the cathedral of the Patriarch of Constantinople, the premier bishop of the eastern Orthodox Church. 'Wisdom' is a favourite title of our Lord, especially in the eastern tradition, but also in Christian thought as a whole. This usage goes back to St Paul's words, 'Christ ... the wisdom of God' (1 Cor 1:24). It was developed by the Church Fathers and found a place in Christian spirituality. The fourteenth century mystic, Henry Suso, called himself 'the servant of Eternal Wisdom' and ardent love for Christ under this title permeates his writings.

The first of the Advent antiphons cries out to Jesus, God's wisdom incarnate and the eternal word of God, who upholds and governs all creation. Advent warns us of the passing nature of this world and all human affairs, not to make us reject creation but to see it in the light of God's purpose. So the antiphons begin with the whole of creation, controlled by divine wisdom, and pray that the conduct of our lives may reflect God's order and beauty.

The 'wisdom' to whom we cry is Jesus himself, but before making that identification we can gain an insight into its full significance by looking briefly at the concept of wisdom in the Old Testament and Apocrypha/Deuterocanonical books, remembering its background in the wider literature of the period.

Every nation has its proverbs, the distilled wisdom of human experience, handed down orally from the distant past and with no known author. Proverbs need not, and usually do not, express heroic virtue. 'Look before you leap.' 'Honesty is the best policy.' 'Don't count your chickens before they're hatched.' They form a basic groundwork of the art of living, a foundation without which we cannot start out to achieve anything truly worthwhile.

The books of Job, Proverbs, Ecclesiastes, Wisdom and Sirach (Ecclesiasticus) form the main bulk of the wisdom literature in the

Old Testament with the Apocrypha. They include material from ancient sources outside Israel. For example, proverbs of the Egyptian sage Amenemope, who flourished about 1000 BC, are the basis of the section beginning at Proverbs 22:17 in the Old Testament. They also show Greek influence, particularly the Book of Wisdom. However, their overall teaching is dominated by reverence for the one God, as shown in the phrase, 'The fear of the Lord is the beginning of wisdom' which repeatedly occurs, with variations, throughout the literature. The biblical authors saw all their maxims about how to live as forms of devotion to the God who was known by name to his chosen people Israel, the one and only true God of all the earth. Yet just because he is Lord of everything, nothing is outside his control and there is nothing true or good in human wisdom which does not derive from him as its source.

The wisdom which is the concern of the biblical authors is essentially practical. It is shrewdness in the decisions we have to make, good judgement, the ability to make a success of life. Wisdom in this sense is to be distinguished from knowledge and learning. It is not the academic equipment of the scholar who has read many books, but the intelligence of the good counsellor, the person of insight, the reliable family friend whom we turn to in a crisis. Solomon, to whom by conventional literary device many of the wisdom books are attributed, was not so much a learned academic as an intelligent practical man who brought a shrewd mind to life's problems, as when he discovers the real mother of the living child claimed by two harlots (1 Kgs 3:16-28).

While some of the maxims in the wisdom literature are astute advice on how to succeed ('He who gives surety for a stranger will smart for it, for he who hates suretyship is secure.' Prov 11:5) yet their more profound insights are concerned with ends rather than means. They expose the hollowness of many of the things people hanker after – wealth and fame in particular. 'He who loves money will not be satisfied with money' (Ecc 4:10). The explosion of scientific knowledge and the mastery over nature achieved by applied science have given the human race immense resources and power, but raise fearsome problems of what courses of action to follow. We have managed to produced enough nuclear weapons to destroy life on earth several times over. Some parts of the world produce so much food that its storage is an expensive headache while people in other parts are starving. Wisdom challenges technical know-how with the question, 'What is the point of all you are doing?'

Concern with how to succeed leads on to the question of what sort of success is worth seeking, that is, concern with ends and values. Values are matters of great practical importance, determine the things we seek and give us an overview or general strategy for the conduct of our lives. In this way, they widen our view from what is of use to us to what is good in itself. In other words, our practical concern with what is most important leads on beyond the practical to consideration of reality for its own sake, a speculative concern.

It is often stated that among the ancient peoples only the Greeks were interested in knowledge as such, apart from its practical application. The ancient Egyptians are said to have commented that the Greeks are like children, they are always asking 'Why?' Whether influenced by the Greeks or not, the biblical authors of the wisdom literature proceeded to consider wisdom itself and its relation to God. The nature psalms express wonder at the created universe and see it as the work of divine wisdom: 'Lord how manifold are thy works! In wisdom hast thou made them all; the earth is full of thy creatures' (Ps 104:24). Similarly, the author of Proverbs writes 'The Lord by wisdom founded the earth ... '(3:19) In these cases, the force of the word is mainly adverbial; 'wisdom' is simply an expression of the way God has made this world which so fills us with wonder. But it is a small step from that to personify the quality of God's creative action, as when wisdom is represented as pleading with us to follow her and be guided by her (Prov 1:20-33). This passage gives a purely literary personification of wisdom, but it prepares the way for a more substantial understanding, later in the book, where wisdom is described as 'created' by God 'at the beginning of his work' (Prov 8:22) and present with him 'like a master workman' (*ibid* v.30) when he created the world.

The books of Wisdom and Sirach further develop this thought until its high point is reached in the words which form the antiphon. Sirach pictures wisdom speaking in God's heavenly assembly, 'I came forth from the mouth of the Most High' (24:3). Wisdom is God's utterance, his word, which spreads through the universe and inspires the whole human race. 'Alone I have made the circuit of the vault of heaven' (Sir 24:5), '... and in every people and nation I have gotten a possession' (v. 6). God, however, has a special place for Israel in his universal plan: 'The one who created me assigned a place for my tent. And he said, "Make your dwelling in Jacob, and in Israel receive your inheritance"' (v.8). The universal wisdom, God's voice heard faintly or clearly in the hearts of all people, is made known in a special way to the children of Israel who have a particular calling to be the instrument of God's plan for universal salvation.

Sirach identifies wisdom with the law of Moses: 'All this is the book of the covenant of the Most High God, the law which Moses commanded us as an inheritance for the congregation of Jacob' (v.23). The law is basically the ten commandments, showing us how to behave towards God and other people, which is an important aspect of wisdom. The psalmist writes in similar vein, extolling the wisdom of the law, 'Thy commandment makes me wiser than my enemies' (Ps 119:98), and condemning the folly of those who disregard it in their pride, 'Have those who work evil no understanding?' (Ps 53:4). The wicked man shows idiot cunning in piling up wealth by cheating and extortion, and expecting to be happy in the long term.

The book of Wisdom, over a century later than Sirach, perhaps about fifty years before Christ, builds on the earlier literature and strongly affirms the divine nature of wisdom as an attribute of God. The author, speaking as Solomon, recounts the knowledge God has given him, 'For it is he [God] who gave me unerring knowledge of what exists' (7:17), and then states, 'I have learned both what is secret and what is manifest, for wisdom, the fashioner of all things, taught me' (7:21, 22). He repeats the ideas of Proverbs that wisdom is God's agent in creation, and also the teacher of humanity, but in the latter case goes further than Proverbs in regarding wisdom as God in his aspect of teaching us. He goes on to speak of wisdom as almost a distinct mode of being within the Godhead, 'For she is a breath of the power of God, and a pure emanation of the glory of the Almighty ... a reflection of eternal light, a spotless mirror of the working of God, and an image of his goodness' (7:25,26). (The pronoun 'she' is a consequence of the Greek word for wisdom, *sophia*, being feminine.) Wisdom, God's image, is the basis of cosmic order, the divine principle which holds the universe in being and keeps it on course in all its change and movement. 'She reaches mightily from one end of the earth to the other, and she orders all things well' (8:1, the verse which forms part of the antiphon).

Wisdom has some resemblance to the concept of the *logos* in Greek Stoic philosophy, which is a rational principle of order governing the universe. God created a cosmos, not a chaos. The fact that science is possible, that the workings of the universe can be studied and described rationally, though the process of discovery is never complete, is an awe-inspiring fact.

Wisdom, in the book of that title, is often associated with God's Spirit. 'Who has learned thy counsel, unless thou hast given wisdom and sent thy holy Spirit from on high?' (9:17). 'She passes into holy souls and makes them friends of God and prophets' (7:27) – a function usually attributed in the Bible to God's Spirit. There is a rich variety of terminology in which to describe the working of God and various terms overlap, warning us against adopting a rigid, inflexible scheme.

The concept of wisdom and its characteristics as developed in the wisdom literature, along with 'Word' (*logos*) and other terms, were available to the early Christians in their attempt to convey the reality of Christ and the mystery of his incarnation. The statement 'I came forth from the mouth of the Most High' (Sir 24:3) conveys the same idea as that found in the concept of the Word which is developed in the prologue of St John's gospel (1:1-14). God's utterance or word is divine in nature, co-eternal with God, his agent in creation, 'the true light that enlightens every man' and the one who became incarnate in Jesus Christ. These ideas echo and fill out the description of wisdom found in Sirach which we noted. Though there is no concept of incarnation in Sirach, yet there is one remarkable verbal similarity to St John's statement 'the Word became flesh and dwelt among us.' 'Dwelt' (Greek *eskénósen*, literally, dwelt as in a tent, *skéné*, that is, for a time) is the language of Sirach 24:8: 'The one who created me assigned a place for my tent. And he said, 'Make your dwelling (*kataskénóson*) in Jacob.' So the cry 'O Wisdom' is suitable as a prayer for the coming of the incarnate Lord which is celebrated in the *Magnificat*.

The Book of Wisdom, however, provides even more of the vocabulary used of Christ in the New Testament. St Paul describes Christ as 'the image of the invisible God' (Col 1:15) who 'is before all things, and in him all things hold together' (v. 17). The epistle to the Hebrews states that God's Son 'reflects the glory of God and bears the very stamp of his nature, upholding the universe by his word of power' (1:3). The words of both authors clearly go back to Wisdom, 'For she is a reflection of eternal light, a spotless mirror of the working of God, and an image of his goodness' (7:26) and 'Wisdom reacheth from one to another mightily: and sweetly doth she order all things' (8:1, *AV*, the words quoted in the antiphon). We have here a link with the Stoic concept of the *logos*, the basic rational principle which upholds the created order and governs its working according to reason. There is also an aesthetic element in wisdom's function as the sustainer of creation, 'mightily and sweetly ordering all things', *fortiter suaviterque disponens omnia*. The words superbly convey the strength and beauty of the cosmos and lead us to adoration. They have a parallel in human behaviour, reminding us of the Latin tag, *fortiter in re, suaviter in modo*, 'firm in principle but flexible, considerate and gentle in its application'.

The connection between the ordered beauty of the heavenly bodies in their movements and the moral beauty of a good life has often been made. Wordsworth apostrophises duty in his Ode:

> Thou dost preserve the stars from wrong;
> And the most ancient heavens, through thee, are fresh and strong.

Kant begins the concluding section of his *Critique of Practical Reason* with the words:

> Two things fill the mind with ever new and increasing admiration and awe, the oftener and the more steadily we reflect on them: *The starry heavens above and the moral law within* .
> (T.K. Abbot's translation, 1883, p.260)

Much earlier, Psalm 19 considers how 'the heavens declare the glory of God' and moves naturally, without any sense of change in subject matter, to the law of God which shines with moral beauty, gives 'wisdom to the simple', 'rejoice(s) the heart', is 'more to be desired than gold' and is 'sweeter than honey'.

Terms used of wisdom in the Old Testament and Apocrypha are applied to Christ in the New, and in a few places the identification between wisdom and Christ become explicit. St Paul writes:

> For Jews demand signs and Greeks seek wisdom but we preach Christ crucified, a stumbling block to Jews and folly to Gentiles but to those who are called, both Jews and Greeks, Christ the power of God and the wisdom of God (1 Cor 1:22-24).

Paul contrasts the pretentious, showy wisdom which delighted the Greeks with the true wisdom which is Christ, which the 'Greeks seek' even though they are so wrong about its nature. There is a parallel here with the thought of the *Magnificat* that the mighty are thrown down and the humble raised up, the needy satisfied and the rich sent empty away. Mary herself exemplifies the wisdom of the humble because she fully realises that her great and unique vocation is solely due to God's grace and her fame to all generations is the result of the mighty work of God her Saviour. Specially endowed by God with the gift of wisdom she is fitted by him to be the bearer of the divine wisdom incarnate.

We pray then, in the antiphon, to Christ under his title of the wisdom of God and ask him to come to us. He is our heart's desire, the one we long for, who satisfies our deepest need. He is God's agent in creation and the unifying principle which holds the universe together. He inspires all that is true and good in human thought and nothing in the life and history of the world's peoples is beyond his concern. When we think of Christ as wisdom it is natural to ask him to 'come and teach us'. Later we shall look at the more frequent petition in the antiphons, 'come and deliver us,' but we can see our need to be delivered more clearly when we are taught by God what he expects of us. The moral law with which Sirach identifies wisdom is in St Paul's words 'our custodian, *paidagógos*, to bring us to Christ' our Saviour (Gal 3:24). Christ shows us the need which he himself meets.

But what we ask Christ to teach us, 'the way of prudence', seems rather an anti-climax after the exalted language we have been using of divine wisdom up to now. 'Prudence' sounds slightly archaic in modern English and conveys a sense of caution, safe investments and careful planning for the future. We need to recapture the full vigour of prudence as one of the four cardinal virtues in moral theology. The cardinal or natural virtues – prudence, temperance, courage and justice – are qualities of behaviour which anyone can see are necessary and right for human beings whether they believe in God or not, in contrast to the theological virtues – faith, hope and love – which explicitly relate us to God in our behaviour. The Christian is first of all a human being and is a very bad Christian if he neglects the ordinary human virtues. Christ did not teach a totally new morality but reminded people of the duties they had already learned, and extended them. He sometimes challenged conventional wisdom, but by no means rejected it out of hand. Most of his teaching shows a robust common sense, appealing to his hearers to use their intelligence and drawing their attention to things they could have known if they stopped to think. The sermon on the mount is full of this homely wisdom, such as, settle your disputes out of court, you can't serve two masters, and, if you with all your faults give good gifts to your children how much more will your heavenly Father attend to your requests? Christ built on what had been taught in the past, taking for granted the basic moral teaching which forms the ground floor of Christian ethics. The upper stories rest on this foundation.

Prudence is a necessary ingredient in all virtuous actions; its absence either seriously reduces their value or nullifies them completely. Prudence means the exercise of our reason in how we act so that the result will be good. It is being responsible to God in the use of our mental powers, whatever their extent. As C.S. Lewis trenchantly states, 'The proper motto is not "Be good, sweet maid, and let who can be clever", but "Be good, sweet maid, and don't forget that this involves being as clever as you can"' (*Mere Christianity*, p.72). Clearly, the best-intentioned acts can be useless or even harmful unless accompanied by a wise assessment of what is required, or more bluntly, by common sense and 'gumption'. The command to love one's neighbour as oneself includes the obligation to think out what is best for one's neighbour and oneself and the right or most effective way to achieve that. Through no fault of our own, our best efforts sometimes fail, and then we remember 'It's the thought that counts.' But that is only a consolation if the attempt to help has been a genuine one in the first place.

The prayer for prudence brings us full circle to the original concern of the wisdom literature – practical directions on how to live. The Advent cry to Christ, the eternal wisdom, to come and teach us the way of prudence is no escape from the real world and its problems, but a proper awareness of this world and how we ought to live in it in the light of God's purpose for creation and for ourselves. Modern versions of the antiphon make this point in its most general form: 'Come and teach us the way of truth' (Roman Catholic and Church of England), or 'Come and teach us how to live' (Anglican Church of Canada). Advent reminds us that this world will come to an end, but that is no reason for neglecting daily duties. On the contrary, the eternal setting of our human life makes what we do here on earth all the more important because our actions have eternal consequences. The way we behave towards God and other people, and the kind of place we make this world to be, are not things which fade into oblivion but are judged, purified and transformed, and what is good in them is taken up into God's perfect kingdom. 'Come, O Wisdom, and teach us how to live.'

CHAPTER 3

O Adonai

O Adonai and Leader of the house of Israel, who appearedst in the bush to Moses in a flame of fire, and gavest him the Law in Sinai: Come and deliver us with an outstretched arm.

O come, O come, thou Lord of might,
Who to thy tribes, on Sinai's height,
In ancient times didst give the law
In cloud and majesty and awe.

And the angel of the LORD appeared to him in a flame of fire out of the midst of a bush (Ex 3:2).

I will redeem you with an outstretched arm (Ex 6:6).

'Adonai' is the Hebrew word for 'Lord'. God has a personal name in the Bible but it was considered too holy for normal use, so when the reader at public worship in the synagogue found the holy name in the text, he read the word 'Adonai', 'Lord', instead. The original text of the Hebrew Bible was written in consonants only and the name of God occurs as YHWH so that its pronunciation can only be guessed. In modern English versions, the sacred name in the Hebrew is usually rendered by 'LORD' in capital letters and in this way we follow the reverence of our Jewish ancestors in the faith by using a word which points to, rather than utters, the holy name of God. 'Adonai' in the antiphon serves the same purpose. It was probably suggested by the Vulgate translation of Exodus 6:3 which retains this Hebrew word in the Latin, ' ... *et nomen meum ADONAI non indicavi eis*' ('but by my name the LORD I did not make myself known to them.') The Latin hymn based on the antiphons also retains the word 'Adonai' – '*Veni, veni Adonai!*' It is kept in Lacey's translation of the hymn and in the prose versions of the *English Hymnal* and the modern Roman Catholic office book. There is a certain numinous awe in the Hebrew word which well conveys the tone and atmosphere of the antiphon. 'Lord of lords' and 'Lord of might' attempt to do the same thing but not quite so successfully.

The name of God which is rendered 'Lord' is associated with the description of God as 'I am who I am' in the account of God's appearance to Moses in the burning bush. Moses was reluctant to undertake the mission of leading the children of Israel out of Egypt, and objected that the people would not believe that God had really appeared to him. What should he answer when they asked him what is God's name? God replied, 'I am who I am' and went on to instruct Moses to tell the people, 'The LORD (YHWH) ... has sent me to you. ' The designations 'Lord' and 'I am' indicate that God is both known to us and beyond our knowledge. He gives us his name, yet this name directs our attention to God as he is in himself, rather than any ideas we may have of him. He is *I am*, not anything we can define or capture in human concepts. So we cry in the antiphon, 'O Adonai, ... come,' not with any power to

34

manipulate God or compel him by knowing his name, but adoring his transcendent majesty and asking him with childlike trust to come and help us.

The first antiphon, O Sapientia, is clearly addressed to Christ, though mainly in his eternal being as the Word, God's agent in creation and the one who upholds the universe. To whom is 'Adonai' addressed? The words which follow suggest that it is God the Father, God as he was known to Israel before Christ, since they refer to the 'leader of the house of Israel', the burning bush and the giving of the law on Sinai. Yet the term 'Lord' (Greek, kurios) is given frequently to Jesus in the New Testament and by Christians ever since. Sometimes it has little more force than 'Sir', but Greek-speaking Jews and Christians were familiar with kurios as the way the divine name was rendered in the Greek translation of the Jewish Scriptures, the Septuagint. So while 'Adonai' is primarily addressed to God the Father, a reference to Christ need not be excluded, just as 'the house of Israel' can also refer to the followers of Christ whom St Paul calls 'the Israel of God' (Gal 6:16). In fact the term's lack of precision is helpful to the antiphon's devotional use as we adore God and Christ together, God as revealed in Christ, without analysing our prayers as to which person of the Trinity they are directed. All the antiphons have this valuable ambiguity. Sometimes the primary reference is to God the Father, as in the present case. More often it is to God the Son, but there is always a close association between the persons of the Trinity.

The antiphon goes on to pray to the 'Leader of the house of Israel'. 'Leader' is not an explicit title of God in the Bible but the idea of leading is very frequent. It is found in the figure of the shepherd, which in the Old Testament is applied to God and his agents, and in the New Testament to Christ also. The Israelites were shepherds in their early history and continued to care for flocks and herds after they had settled in the promised land and became predominantly cultivators of the soil. An eastern shepherd would normally walk in front of his flocks, leading them. Here, ready to hand, was a familiar picture to show God's loving care of his people, as seen especially in the best known of the Psalms where we say of God 'He leads me beside still waters, ... in the paths of righteousness' (Ps 23:2,3).

The figure of the shepherd, with its rich associations, which is applied to God in the Old Testament, is represented in St John's gospel as belonging to Jesus, the good shepherd who 'calls his own sheep by name and leads them out' (Jn 10:3). 'He goes before them, and the sheep follow him, for they know his voice' (v.4). Christ our shepherd gives us a sense of direction and answers our need for leadership in a confusing and dangerous world. 'Give us a lead' is often a cry from the heart, whether or not it is put into words. People demand leadership from their politicians; teenagers follow with adulation their pop-star idols. We hanker for direction and goals with which we can identify, and we are willing to make sacrifices if we are convinced that our leaders are trustworthy and the objectives they put before us worthwhile.

This antiphon presents the God revealed in Jesus Christ as the ultimate answer to the world's needs for leadership. The wisdom which 'mightily and sweetly ordereth all things' does not override our freedom or force us into a particular line of conduct. God leads us but does not drive us. We follow his leading, not because we have to, but because it appeals to those urges in our nature which we judge to be deepest and best. Our Christian faith is that God is sovereign Lord over all creation, yet his leadership is not like the heavy hand of a totalitarian state. His supreme rule is known only by faith, not with the coercive evidence of logical demonstration. We have the choice to accept or reject his rule, but if we accept it then we commit ourselves to him as Lord and make all other concerns subordinate to God's kingdom and judge every human claim to leadership by the criterion of God's will.

The thought of God as leader, and our crying need for leadership, recurs in the antiphons. We shall meet it again when considering 'the root of Jesse' which is an 'ensign' to the peoples, pointing out the way of life. Also, when we think of Christ as 'King of the nations' we shall see that he is a shepherd king who does not dominate his people but gently leads them in the paths of righteousness.

'O Adonai and Leader of the house of Israel, who appearedst in the bush to Moses in a flame of fire ...' We noted earlier that God's appearance to Moses in the burning bush is associated with the sacred name indicated by 'Adonai' and God's self-description as 'I am who I am'. The burning bush, which cannot be preserved as an idol, is an appropriate symbol of the God who goes before us, leads us, but is beyond our grasp and not in our power. When he heard God speak from the bush 'Moses hid his face, for he was afraid to look at God' (Ex 3:6). The last antiphon, *O Emmanuel*, speaks of a God who is intimate and close to us, but the full glory of this fact is missed if we forget the immense distance between sinful man and God most holy, which only God himself can bridge. Awe, and even terror, is a necessary part of our attitude to God. The unknown author of Hebrews tells us 'Our God is a consuming fire' (12:29). His will is that we should be perfect, purified from all dross, like precious silver and gold. God created us in his own image and likeness, that is, to be finite mirrors of infinite perfection, and the re-creation of the human race is the restoration in us of the divine image which has been tarnished and spoilt by human sin. If we are to find the eternal happiness which is God's will for us, everything contrary to that will must be consumed in the fire of his love so that only the pure metal remains. The bush which burned but was not consumed is an apt figure of God's purifying love fashioning us into creatures who can live for ever in the brightness of his presence. The mystics like to speak of God's love in terms of fire, as in the title of Gerlac Petersen's classic, *The Fiery Soliloquy with God*. His older contemporary, Jan van Ruysbroeck (1293-1381), thought of union with God as 'every soul like a live coal, burned up by God on the heart of His Infinite Love' (quoted in Evelyn Underhill's *Mysticism*, p.421).

It is not accidental that fire is regarded as holy in many religions, from the sacred fire tended by the vestal virgins in ancient Rome and the fire ritual in Zoroastrianism, to the paschal fire by which Christians greet the resurrection of Christ. The fearsome power of fire is a fit symbol of the awe and majesty of God, when combined with other symbols showing his gentler aspects to correct any one-sided emphasis on power.

The God who appeared to Moses in the burning bush is also the God who 'gave him the law on Sinai'. The burning bush appearance occurred when God first called Moses to lead the chosen people out of Egypt. The giving of the law happened after a long, dangerous and difficult struggle with the Egyptians from whom God had freed his people and brought them some way to the promised land. Both events occurred in the same place, Sinai or Horeb, different names for the same mountain. Moses was filled with holy dread when God spoke to him out of the burning bush. The giving of the law on Sinai was accompanied by the cloud of God's presence, by terrifying sights and sounds and a stern warning to the people not to come near the holy mountain lest they die (Ex 19:16-25). The description of these terrors sounds to modern ears like the account of a thunderstorm, earthquake and volcanic eruption all in one, but to speak in those terms is to miss the point of the passage. Awe in the presence of a great mystery beyond human understanding, *mysterium tremendum et fascinans*, is the meaning intended, not mere physical fear of natural phenomena which can be measured on the Richter scale or the meteorologist's chart. The moral law given in the ten commandments comes to us with a force and demand which make us acknowledge its divine origin and bow in reverence before the one who gave it, our mighty Lord and judge. *O Adonai* well interprets the words of the Magnificat

> For he that is mighty hath magnified me:
> and holy is his name.

J.M. Neale also captures the sense in the line he translates, 'in cloud, and majesty and awe.'

The account in Exodus of the giving of the law, expressed in the

38

language of rich symbolism and not of literalistic history, stresses above all the divine origin of the moral law. It need disturb no one that close similarities to the ten commandments are found in sources outside Israel, such as the code of Hammurabi in ancient Babylon, long before the time of Moses. The God who revealed his will specially to the chosen people also made it known to the human race as a whole, however much this knowledge is suppressed and distorted by human sin. The demands of conscience, even though conscience needs to be developed and taught, are heard in varying degrees by everybody and are the mark of God in the human soul. Attempts have been made to give a purely natural account of our moral sense but they fail to carry widespread conviction. For many people, moral demands open a window from the purely material order to a realm of values which can lead them to God.

However, the main emphasis in the antiphon is on the law as given in God's special revelation of himself. Our sense of right and wrong is deepened and sharpened when we see it as springing from the nature of God, as required by God and as an obligation to a personal God who loves us, cares for us and wills our eternal well-being. St Paul speaks of the law as 'our custodian until Christ came' (Gal 3:24) and emphasises that it is not the means of salvation but shows up in stark clarity our moral bankruptcy. The law by itself would fill us with despair as no one has succeeded in keeping it fully. Yet without the moral law we would not see our need for a Saviour. The law is not on its own but is part of the revelation of God's love, his will for us his children as forgiven sinners in communion with him. The first commandment is introduced by the statement that God had rescued his people from slavery. 'I am the LORD your God, who brought you out of the land of Egypt, out of the house of bondage. You shall have no other gods before me' (Ex 20:2,3). Before God gave his people the ten commandments, he freed them from their chains. God's grace comes before our obedience and makes obedience a matter of joyful gratitude. The characteristic feature of Christian ethics – that doing good is a response of love and gratitude to God's loving action in

Christ's salvation – is already foreshadowed in the giving of the ten commandments to Moses *after* God, the 'leader of the house of Israel', had brought his people out of Egypt.

The petition of the antiphon, 'Come and redeem us with thy outstretched arm', asks God, in the typical fashion of the Bible, to do what he has already done. 'Outstretched arm' is a fixed epithet in the Bible, like 'wine-dark sea' in Homer, for God's mighty deliverance of Israel from Egyptian bondage. God promised the Israelites through Moses 'I will redeem you with an outstretched arm' (Ex 6:6) and the phrase is frequently used to describe the past event in order to encourage the people to obey and trust God in the present and future. 'The LORD your God brought you out thence with a mighty hand and an outstretched arm; therefore the LORD your God commanded you to keep the sabbath day' (Deut 5:15). 'You shall remember ... the mighty hand and outstretched arm, by which the LORD your God brought you out; so will the LORD your God do to all the peoples of whom you are afraid' (Deut 7:18,19). God *has* delivered us; therefore we can be confident he will deliver us in the future. That confidence is the basis of our Advent prayer, 'Come and deliver us with an outstretched arm.'

The bondage of the Israelites in Egypt is a parable of all that enslaves God's children in every age and place. We pray for ourselves and for the whole human family, that God will free us because he has freed us. The cry of all who groan under the yoke of poverty or disease, of political oppression and economic exploitation, of ignorance, lack of opportunity and above all of universal human sin, is offered to God in the prayer for the coming of the Saviour who has come. Freedom from bondage is a theme running through the antiphons. We shall meet it again when we consider the key of David and the Day-spring whom we ask to deliver us from the prison of darkness and the shadow of death.

In the Old Testament the phrase 'with an outstretched arm' is a metaphor of strength, the power which drove back the Red Sea and stopped the river Jordan so that God's people could escape their enemies and enter the promised land. But since Christ came, the words take on a more wonderful and unexpected meaning because we cannot forget that Christ stretched out his arms on the cross to deliver us from the bondage of evil in all its forms. At first sight, this act of deliverance is the exact opposite of the rescue from Egypt, weakness instead of strength, but the cross shows the power of suffering love. An Indian blessing, the *Christaraksha*, makes this point in striking language:

> May the cross of the Son of God, who is mightier
> than all the hosts of Satan, and more glorious
> than all the angels of heaven, abide with you in
> your going out and your coming in! By day and by
> night, at morning and at evening, at all times and
> in all places, may it protect and defend you!
> From the wrath of evil men, from the assaults of
> evil spirits, from foes visible and invisible,
> from the snares of the devil, from all low passions
> that beguile the soul and body, may it guard,
> protect, and deliver you. Amen.

The Christ who was crucified in weakness is supreme over all creation. Mary's words in the *Magnificat*, 'he hath showed strength with his arm', celebrate the victory of the weak and lowly over arrogant might. The proud empire of Caesar gives way before the kingdom of God, manifest in a baby in a manger and a Saviour on a cross. We pray in Advent to the Christ who has redeemed the world by his cross, that the fruits of his redemption may be revealed in all creation. 'Come and deliver us with an outstretched arm.'

CHAPTER 4

O Root of Jesse

O Radix Jesse. O Root of Jesse, which standest for an ensign of the people, at whom kings shall shut their mouths, to whom the Gentiles shall seek: Come and deliver us, and tarry not.

O come, thou Rod of Jesse, free
Thine own from Satan's tyranny;
From depths of hell thy people save,
And give them victory o'er the grave.

The root of Jesse shall stand as an ensign to the peoples; him shall the nations seek (Is 11:10).

Kings shall shut their mouths because of him (Is 52:15).

I shall bring near my deliverance, it is not far off, and my salvation will not tarry (Is 46:13).

The Christ whom we pray to come and deliver us is the Saviour of the whole world and also the product of a particular nation with its own special culture and traditions. The antiphon *O Radix Jesse* brings out both the rootedness of Christ in Israel and his significance for all mankind. He is an 'ensign', *signum*, to all peoples and the one sought by all nations, *gentes*, the Gentiles.

The Jewishness of Jesus is important for understanding his mission to the world. The incarnation of God took place in a true man of flesh and blood with a human ancestry, a country, a mother tongue, a local, temporal existence. Jesus, son of Mary, is the grandson of ..., and great-grandson of ... We could go on tracing the family tree through many generations of Jewish men and women. The human heredity of Jesus is the instrument of God's incarnation. Jesse, a man only remembered because of his famous son, David, is a fitting example of the innumerable obscure people who were ancestors on the human side of God's only Son. The root of Jesse bears the fruit who is the judge and saviour of the world. 'Root' in Isaiah 11:10 is closely connected with 'shoot' in verse 1 where Isaiah says 'There shall come forth a shoot from the stump of Jesse and a branch shall grow out of his roots ... with righteousness he shall judge the poor and decide with equity for the meek of the earth' (Is 11:1, 4). Both the local, national origins of the Messiah and his universal role are here proclaimed.

That God should choose one particular race, and moreover a small and insignificant one, to be the means of his supreme revelation to the world is an offence, an obstacle for faith, to many people both ancient and modern. Celsus, the third century critic of the Christian message, asked why God should specially reveal himself to Jews and Christians. 'If God ... determined to rescue mankind from evil, why on earth did he send this spirit into one particular corner? He ought to have breathed through many bodies in the same way and sent them all over the world' (quoted in T.R. Glover, *The Conflict of Religions in the Roman World* p. 249). The 'scandal of particularity' is an offence to human wisdom, but when it is pondered it opens up an insight into God's gracious method of choosing the weak and unworthy to be the particular channels of his mercy to all the world. Those whom God chooses are not to be proud because they are chosen, or contemptuous of others (Deut 7:7, 9:4), but to realise that their weakness and unworthiness highlight the sheer gift-love of God. He takes those with least pretensions as a pilot project in his plan to bring all peoples to himself so that they may know him and love him.

Not only did God choose a small, obscure nation for his special people, but within that nation he fulfilled his purpose through a small remnant. The root of Jesse, in Isaiah 11, refers to a nation devastated and its royal family reduced to a cut-down tree stump. Yet out of a small and faithful nucleus, God ensured the future of his people with its calling, in the fulness of time, to be his instrument for the salvation of the world. The Messiah when he came, though of the royal line of David, was not a member of the political or religious establishment in Israel, but was born in a carpenter's family and spent most of his adult life on earth as an artisan. 'The root of Jesse' as a title of the Messiah has a whole background of God's choice of the poor and the lowly, the faithful remnant who are left in a weakened state when the majority of the people disappear through their faithlessness. When we use the antiphon to invoke our Lord as 'the root of Jesse', and cry to him to 'come and deliver us', we are taught that God effects the world's salvation through a mighty act of grace by using those who are without power in a worldly sense, culminating in the powerlessness of the cross. The antiphon again illustrates the paradox, which runs through the *Magnificat*, of God's almighty power embodied in the meek and lowly.

Some English versions of the antiphons speak of the 'rod' or 'shoot' of Jesse, picking up the word *virgula*, 'twig', in the Latin hymn and connecting 'root' in Isaiah 11:10 with 'rod' in verse 1. Probably the two words in Isaiah refer to the same person, but it may not be too fanciful to read into them the truth that Christ is not only the product of Israel's history, but also its source and origin. The author of Revelation hears Christ say, 'I am the root and offspring of David' (22:16). Christ is both son of David and also his Lord (Mk 12:35-37). Just as Christ, the eternal Word and the one through whom the universe was made, became part of his own creation, so he who is the fruit of the chosen people is also the root from which that people derived its life.

'The root of Jesse' calls to mind a common motif in Christian art, the Jesse tree, found in stained glass windows, carvings in metal or stone and sometimes shaped into candelabra. Jesse trees, along with Advent wreaths, have been used effectively in many churches to bring home the meaning of the season in a visible form. To depict the genealogy of Jesus in the shape of a tree clearly shows his rootedness in the history of the chosen people and strengthens the words of the *Magnificat*:

> He has come to the help of his servant Israel:
> for he has remembered his promise of mercy,
> the promise he made to our fathers:
> to Abraham and his children for ever.

'Tree' is a figure which meets us at significant points in the Bible story, all of which contribute to our understanding of this antiphon. The tree of life was planted in the Garden of Eden, but Adam and Eve lost the benefit of it because they ate from the tree of the knowledge of good and evil. Christ reversed Adam's fall by suffering death on the cross, which is sometimes described as a tree (e.g. 1 Peter 2:24). As a result, the tree of life is again available to human beings. In Revelation, the risen Christ promises the faithful in Ephesus, 'To him who conquers I will grant to eat of the tree of life' (2:7) whose leaves are described later in the book as 'for the healing of the nations' (22:2). The latter phrase links this figure with the 'sun of righteousness' in *O Oriens* which arises 'with healing in his wings'. There is a whole cluster of associations which gives depth and power to our cry to the coming Lord under the title 'root of Jesse'.

St Matthew begins his gospel with the family tree of Jesus from Abraham onwards, to show how the Messiah is rooted in the people of Israel and fulfils their history. St Luke also gives the genealogy of Christ but he traces his roots right back to Adam. The particular reality of Jesus means that he belongs to one nation, one people. He spent most of his time in the flesh in one small area of the earth's surface, at a precise time in the world's history, from the reign of Augustus Caesar to that of Tiberius. It is this particularity of Jesus that the title 'root of Jesse' primarily conveys. Yet the word 'root' also reminds us that Jesus is fully part of the whole human family. Following St Luke, we can claim that he belongs not only to Israel but to all of us. He is bone of our bone and flesh of our flesh, and his universal significance is proclaimed by the rest of the antiphon.

Christ, the root of Jesse, stands 'as an ensign to the peoples; him shall the nations seek'. Isaiah no doubt referred primarily to the return of Jewish exiles to a politically free Israel. 'He will raise an ensign for the nations, and will assemble the outcasts of Israel, and gather the dispersed of Judah from the four corners of the earth' (11:12). The exiles think back with longing to the golden age of king David and the prophet's message gives them hope that a new David will appear and guide them to the promised land. He will be an 'ensign', a signpost showing them the way. But in the prophetic oracle, this sign is not simply one for exiled Jews pointing to their political freedom. 'Him shall the nations seek.' The new Davidic king will be a rallying point for the world's nations looking for assurance and direction in their own future.

The words of Isaiah are fulfilled in Christ. What the land of Israel means to a Jewish exile is a parable of every human being's longing for communion with the God and Father of us all. Many people think that life is pointless; they have become disillusioned and cynical, perhaps because their youthful idealism has been derided and betrayed, and they mock any higher aim than material self-interest. But everyone has a homing instinct for God which our sinful, fallen nature has not totally destroyed. Christ is a sign to the world, guiding all people to their true homeland, bringing them into fellowship with God and reconciling them to one another. That is what St Paul understood when he argued that Christ is saviour of both Jews and Gentiles, quoting Isaiah's words in the rather different form given in the Greek version of the Hebrew Bible, 'and further Isaiah says, "The root of Jesse shall come, he who rises to rule the Gentiles; in him shall the Gentiles hope"' (Rom 15:12).

Consciously or unconsciously, the Gentiles 'seek' Christ. The word 'seek' in its original context can have the sense of consulting an oracle, a frequent practice in the ancient world and found among the Jews who turned to God for guidance in perplexing situations. In an age of great uncertainty and rapid change, it is tempting to listen to the loudest voice, the most authoritative pronouncement and bombastic claim. A dazed and frightened people can easily fall victim to doctrinaire, totalitarian systems of both the religious and political variety. Christ is not that kind of sign to the world's peoples; his leadership frees rather than enslaves because he treats us as free, responsible beings who can respond to his call and step out in faith, not knowing what the future holds but trusting in his continuing guidance and care. This kind of leadership leaves us with many unanswered questions but it is the authentic sign to the world. The description 'an ensign of the people' links up with 'leader of the house of Israel' in *O Adonai* and expresses the same quality of 'mightily and sweetly ordering all things' found in *O Sapientia*.

Direction, however, is not always enough when we find ourselves in dangerous and difficult circumstances. We often need help as well as advice, and the word 'seek' in the antiphon can include the sense of a cry for help. The version in the Canadian Service Book reads, 'all peoples will summon you to their aid'. Christ is both sign and support to a world floundering in a morass of perplexity, temptation and moral weakness. Christ shows us the road, one step at a time, and helps us along.

'The root of Jesse shall stand as an ensign to the peoples: him shall the nations seek.' The antiphon inserts in this verse the clause, 'at whom kings shall shut their mouths' (Is 52:15), which comes from the last of the suffering servant songs in the second part of Isaiah, generally accepted as written by a later, anonymous prophet. These songs have had a great influence on our understanding of Christ's work of salvation through the suffering and degradation of the cross. The whole of the last song (Is 52:13-53:12) depicts God's servant as the innocent, uncomplaining victim who suffers oppression, shame and disease, and yet in the end is raised up by God to a position of honour and success. The servant bears his undeserved sufferings willingly as the burden of the people's sin which he takes on himself, and by doing so brings healing and forgiveness to the many who have sinned.

The words 'at whom kings shall shut their mouths' refer to the horror which the servant's tortured body produces in the minds of the world's rulers when they see him. They are struck dumb by the hideous scars, or the ravages of a disfiguring disease which are plainly evident on his face. Some forms of suffering excite revulsion as well as pity. The *New English Bible* translates the phrase, 'kings curl their lips in disgust'.

This reference to the shame and suffering of the Messiah – the only one in the antiphons – cannot be too highly valued. The desire of the world for meaning can only be met by a Saviour who identifies with us sinful, suffering human beings, shares our rejection and alienation from God and, by his willing acceptance of human misery, brings us back to fellowship with God. The Old Testament conception of the coming deliverer as a mighty lord would be glaringly incomplete without the utter self-giving of the suffering servant. The only hope for the world lies in the rejection of the worldly values of pride and self-seeking by a radical act of love, obedient even to death.

Probably no Jew up to the time of Christ identified the suffering servant in Isaiah with the Messiah. The servant represented for them Israel in the misfortune of its chequered history, but the Messiah was expected to be a mighty warrior who would deliver them from their sufferings. Christ, in his life and passion, brings together the figures of suffering servant and triumphant Messiah.

The coming one is greater than the hopes and ideas of those who dimly foresaw his coming.

With the thoughts in our minds of a Saviour who is rooted in Israel's history, who is a guide and help to a distracted world, and who shoulders the sufferings produced by the world's sin and folly, we can go on to pray with eager longing, 'Come and deliver us, and tarry not.' There is a child-like note in the last two words. Children want things *now*; they find it hard to wait. Their eagerness often prevents them from being polite in their requests. The same child-like rudeness to God is found many times in the Psalms in prayers which reproach God for his neglect of his people ('Thou hast made us a byword among the nations', 44:14), and vigorously plead with him for help ('Rouse thyself! ... Awake! Do not cast us off for ever!' 44:23). The picture that comes to mind is of a child tugging at his mother's dress when she is busy, to try and attract her attention to some pressing matter of his own. Reading the Bible as whole, and especially our Lord's words, we cannot doubt that this eagerness to the point of rudeness is pleasing to God. Our prayer, 'Tarry not', is just what he wishes to do, and is another example of that true prayer which asks what God intends to give. The words of Isaiah quoted at the head of this chapter are echoed by Habakkuk:

> For still the vision awaits its time;
> it hastens to the end – it will not lie.
> If it seem slow wait for it;
> it will surely come, it will not delay (2:3).

Waiting for God to fulfil his plans in his own good time does not mean a listless resignation towards the troubles of the present, but is fully compatible with an eager pleading with God to come and deliver us, soon.

In the parable of the importunate widow and the unjust judge, the widow's pleading illustrates the mood of the antiphon. She was probably cheated by someone powerful in the community; she knows she has a good case and, even if the judge is a hard, unfeeling and unprincipled man, she will pester him until he gives her justice. This is one of the parables of contrast; Jesus is saying that God is *not* like the unjust judge. 'Hear what the unrighteous judge says. And will not God vindicate his elect, who cry to him day and night? Will he delay long over them? I tell you he will vindicate them speedily' (Lk 18:6-8). Jesus argues, *a fortiori*, that if even someone as unsympathetic as this judge can be persuaded to grant the widow's persistent request, how much more will God respond to the prayers of his faithful people. There is no doubt about God's willingness to act for our good. The only doubt is whether we are willing to receive what he wills to give us. 'Nevertheless, when the Son of Man comes, will he find faith on earth?' (v.8). St Augustine's statement quoted earlier is also apposite here: 'God does not ask us to tell him about our needs in order to learn about them, but in order that we may be made capable of receiving his gifts.' The eager prayer, 'Come and deliver us and tarry not', is one of the ways in which we prepare ourselves for Christ's deliverance, because our openness to God is a necessary condition of the working out of his purpose.

'Come and deliver us.' The antiphon does not specify the evils from which we ask to be delivered, but the hymn states them in robust words, 'Satan's tyranny' (*ex hostis ... ungula*, 'from the claw of the enemy'), 'depths of hell' (*de specu Tartari*), 'the grave' (*antro barathri*, 'the cave of the abyss'). The abstract terms we prefer nowadays – alienation, hopelessness, despair – are tame in comparison. God, through Christ, has won and is winning a great victory over the forces of evil and we need the expressive language of concrete metaphor, and even myth, to bring home the fact to our feelings and imagination. This century has seen the horrors of Auchtwitz, the Stalinist purges, the killing fields of Pol Pot. The depths of human depravity, which these atrocities reveal to our startled minds, show a more than human dimension to the evil in the world. We can only appreciate the wonder of God's deliverance if we take to heart the magnitude of the evil from which he sets us free. 'Come and deliver us, tarry not.'

CHAPTER 5

O Key of David

O Clavis David. O Key of David, and Sceptre of the house of Israel; that openest and no man shutteth, and shuttest, and no man openeth: Come and bring the prisoner out of the prison-house, and him that sitteth in darkness and the shadow of death.

O come, thou Key of David, come,
And open wide our heavenly home:
Make safe the way that leads on high,
And close the path to misery.

Who has the key of David, who opens and no one shall shut, who shuts and no one opens (Rev 3:7 cf. Is 22:22).

To bring out the prisoners from the dungeon, from the prison those who sit in darkness (Is 42:7).

A key is widely recognised as a symbol of authority. Twenty-first birthday cards prominently display a door-key, showing that the young adult has the freedom to come and go without asking permission. The Victorian housewife carried a large bunch of keys controlling access to the many rooms, store places and cupboards, to serve the needs of a large family with numerous servants. In ancient times, the key was an even more impressive object of authority. The words of Isaiah on which this antiphon is based read, 'I will place on his shoulder the key of the house of David' (Is 22:22). Such a key 'was an object of considerable size and was proudly carried in public on state occasions' (*Isaiah 1-39*, Commentary by A. S. Herbert, p. 139). In fact it had very much the significance of the sceptre with which it is associated in the antiphon 'O key of David and sceptre of the house of Israel.' These are both royal insignia.

In its original context the key of David was given to Eliakim, a faithful steward of the royal house, in the place of Shebna, the steward who proved unworthy and was deposed from his high office (Is. 22: 15-22). The author of Revelation applies the phrase to our Lord when he speaks to the church in Philadelphia (Rev. 3:7) and it is on this version that the antiphon is most closely based. Christ is described in Revelation as 'the holy one, the true one, who has the key of David, who opens and no one shall shut, who shuts and no one opens.' God's people Israel often proved unfaithful to him, as the prophets lament. They looked back to David as the ideal king and, while castigating the people for their sins which caused their misfortunes, they encouraged them with the hope of a new king David who would rescue them from their plight. This expectation gave the New Testament writers a term to describe Christ. In the book of Revelation, Christ is the one 'who has the key of David'. The antiphon goes a step further in addressing Christ as himself 'the key of David'. We pray to him with longing in Advent to open the doors of our prison house and bring us in to the liberty of the children of God. We pray with faith because we believe he has all authority in heaven and on earth. He is the one 'who opens and no one shall shut, who shuts and no one opens.' The words convey his supreme authority; no one can override what he decides. He is the pioneer of our salvation who, by the mighty acts of his life, death and resurrection, has established his authority over all creation and opened up the way to God for all who are willing to be rescued from a Godless life.

The authority symbolised in the key is closely connected with the forgiveness of sins. 'The power of the keys' is a term for the ministry of absolution. In the fullest sense, only God in Christ can forgive sins, and Christ often combined physical healing with release from sin and guilt, as when he said to the paralysed man, 'My son, your sins are forgiven' (Mk 2:5). Any one can be forgiven by direct prayer to Christ. Yet many find they need the assurance from a fellow-Christian that God has forgiven them. Christ said to Peter, 'I will give you the keys of the kingdom of heaven, and whatever you bind on earth shall be bound in heaven, and whatever you loose on earth shall be loosed in heaven' (Mt 16:19) and he gave the authority to bind and loose to the other apostles also (Mt 18:18). Since we belong with one another in Christ's body, the priest who mediates Christ's forgiveness through the ministry of reconciliation is not coming between the penitent sinner and God, but is helping him receive God's forgiveness more fully. The preacher proclaiming Christ's forgiveness to the penitent as the ambassador of Christ, the priest in public worship pronouncing the absolution, or in the one-to-one situation of the confessional, bring home to the truly repentant the fact that their sins are forgiven by God. Many people need this assurance from the mouth of a fellow human being. Canon Bill Arlow, based in St Anne's Cathedral, Belfast, has worked hard to bring the healing love of Christ to the deeply divided and troubled community in Northern Ireland. Late one night a man knocked at his door. He was a terrorist, distressed almost to the point of suicide by the actions he was involved in. He said 'My conscience is killing me and I want to know one thing – will God forgive me for the things I have done?' Arlow replied, 'God will forgive you and treat you as if you had never sinned if you repent – this is the gospel' (Bill

Arlow, *Over to you*, Christian Journals Ltd 1980, p38.) The terrorist knew, intellectually, that God would forgive him. But for this truth to become a reality in his own experience he needed to hear it from the lips of another person. The 'power of the keys' has made Christ's forgiveness real to many troubled souls.

While 'key of David' is used symbolically to represent the authority of Christ, the rest of the Antiphon takes the phrase to some degree more literally and asks Christ to unlock the prison doors and set free the captives from 'darkness and the shadow of death'. The Advent hymn goes even further and prays that the key may open up the road to heaven and firmly lock the gateway to eternal darkness.

Imprisonment, often unjust, is a feature of life in many ages, including the present when hostages and political prisoners are periodically in the news. The Bible has many examples of innocent prisoners, from Joseph in the Egyptian dungeon, and Jeremiah in the muddy cistern, to Paul in Rome and John the seer in Patmos. This may be partly why consideration for prisoners features so much in the Bible and it should arouse our sympathy in the present violent age when there are so many innocent captives. The Psalmist praises the Lord who 'sets the prisoners free' (146:7). The prophet proclaims God's word, 'Return to your stronghold, O prisoner of hope' (Zech 9:12). The Lord's servant in the servant songs of second Isaiah is appointed as 'a light to the nations to open the eyes that are blind, to bring out the prisoners from the dungeon, from the prison those who sit in darkness' (Is 42: 6,7). God's anointed one (Messiah) is 'to proclaim liberty to the captives, and the opening of the prison to those who are bound' (Is 61:1), words which Jesus applied to himself when he preached in the synagogue of his home town, Nazareth. In the parable of the sheep and the goats, visiting the prisoners is one of the duties one group neglected and the other performed and, in both cases, it is Christ himself who is visited or neglected.

But it would be a mistake to think that God's gift of freedom to prisoners applies only to the innocent. The main point of the gospel is God's love for sinners and offer of salvation to the guilty. When imprisonment is our own fault God is still ready to free us. A familiar prayer in the 1926 Irish Prayer Book petitions God, 'though we be tied and bound with the chain of our sins, yet let the pitifulness of thy great mercy loose us'. The imprisonment here mentioned is the bondage of guilt for past sins, the moral paralysis of bad habits and the besetting sins which hold us in their grip. God's will is the freedom of all who are prisoners in any sense of the word. The physical walls of a prison, the sense of guilt, the helpless feeling in the face of temptation, or the mental fog which hides evil's true nature, the despair and suffering which our sin and folly bring to ourselves and others, are all features of a fallen world. Christ the liberator comes to destroy this bondage in all its forms and set the prisoners free.

Freedom for captives, the correlative to imprisonment, is one of the great themes of the Bible. The phrase, 'who brought you out of the land of Egypt', is one of the most frequent attributes of God in the Old Testament, where this great act of deliverance is a dominating theme. The antiphon O Adonai showed us the continuing power and saving work of the God who brought his people out of Egypt 'with a mighty hand and outstretched arm' and prayed that God would continue to deliver us from every kind of captivity. Through Moses, God not only rescued the people from physical and political slavery, but also made them a nation, gave them a law. The antiphon O Adonai connected God as law giver with God as deliverer. Hence the deliverance from Egypt affected their whole national life profoundly and gave them hope of future deliverance when they were oppressed and exiled. Thus they were to treat kindly those who through poverty had made themselves bond-servants, 'You shall remember that you were a slave in the land of Egypt, and the LORD your God redeemed you' (Deut 15:15).

Captivity and deliverance were a feature of Israel's life even after entry to the promised land. The book of Judges announces with monotonous regularity, 'the children of Israel again did evil in the sight of the LORD and the LORD sold them into the hand of ...'

(4:1, 2. See also 3:7,12; 6:1; 11:1). In each case God sends them a 'judge', a champion, when they cry to him for mercy. Later on in Israel's history, under the kings, the land was often invaded by the armies of one powerful empire after another as they rose and fell in turn. Second only in importance to the deliverance from Egypt was the deportation and return of the exiles from Babylon, which forms the background of the great prophets Jeremiah, Ezekiel and second Isaiah. In all cases political freedom is connected with national repentance and renewal. Ezekiel couples God's promise of a return from exile 'I will take you from the nations ... and bring into your own land'(36:24), with cleansing from sin and the gift of his Spirit 'I will sprinkle clear water over you and you shall be clean from all your uncleanness, and from your idols I will cleanse you' (v.25). 'And I will put my spirit within you' (v.27).

The moral and spiritual dimensions of freedom in the prophets helped prepare for Christ's teaching and for the freedom he won for the world through his death and resurrection. It was at the time of the Passover, the festival of deliverance from Egypt, that he was crucified and the early Church was quick to interpret Christ's victory over evil as a new, more glorious Exodus. When he instituted the sacrament of Holy Communion at the last supper, Christ used words which recall God's covenant made through Moses, 'This is my blood of the covenant which is poured out for many' (Mk 14:24,cf. Ex 24:8). When the Jews celebrated the passover, they sacrificed a lamb and sprinkled its blood on the door posts of their houses. The passover (paschal) lamb became a figure for Christ, crucified and risen. Hence St Paul writes, 'Christ, our paschal lamb, has been sacrificed. Let us, therefore, celebrate the festival' (1 Cor 5:7,8). The name for the festival of the resurrection in most languages is derived from the Aramaic word for Passover, *pascha*. (The English name, 'Easter', is an exception.) The death and resurrection of Christ taken together constitute one great act of freeing the human race from the dominion of sin and death. The Advent prayer, 'Come and free the prisoners,' points forward to the cross and empty tomb.

The universal scope of the freedom Christ's passion brings is illustrated by the tradition that after his death he descended into Hades (*ad infernos*) and 'preached to the spirits in prison' (1 Pet 3:19). These mysterious words have given rise to much speculation about the different stages the soul passes through after death and about the fate of those who died without having heard the gospel of Christ. Is there a period of waiting before the final bliss? Do all those who lived before Christ, or who having lived after him never come into effective contact with his saving message, get a chance to respond to his love in the afterlife? It is futile to expect precise answers to questions such as these. All we can say with certainty about Christ's descent to the realms of the dead is that nothing and no one is beyond the power of God's love, except those who wilfully and finally reject that love. Christ has established his lordship over every age and realm, conquering every evil power and making freedom possible for everyone enslaved to the forces of darkness. The seer in the Book of Revelation heard the glorified Christ say, 'Fear not, I am the first and the last, and the living one; I died, and behold I am alive for evermore, and I have the keys of Death and Hades' (1: 17,18). The authority symbolised by the keys can be helpfully connected with Christ's 'harrowing of hell', opening the doors of the prison house to free the captives and bolting them to stop all but the finally impenitent (if there should be any such) straying from the sphere of God's love.

'Darkness and the shadow of death' are phrases which are specially associated with prison in the Bible. No doubt the physical darkness of ancient dungeons was not the least affliction which prisoners had to bear. Darkness and gloom are common metaphors for the depression, hopelessness and despair which most frequently have been the state of those in prison. The prophet's words are therefore all the more full of hope, 'I have given you as a light to the nations, to open the eyes that are blind, to bring out the prisoners from the dungeon, from the prison those who sit in darkness' (Is 42:6,7).

'The shadow of death' is a phrase often linked with darkness. Further discussion of the combined expression will be postponed till we deal with the antiphon *O Oriens*.

John Bunyan's *The Pilgrim's Progress* describes how Christian and Hopeful found themselves in the grounds of Doubting Castle owned by Giant Despair. The giant captured them and threw them into 'a very dark dungeon' where they languished for some days. Suddenly Christian burst out to his companion, 'What a fool, quoth he, am I thus to lie in a stinking dungeon, when I may as well walk at liberty! I have a key in my bosom, called Promise, that will, I am persuaded, open any lock in Doubting Castle.' The key opened the door of their dungeon, the outer door in the castle yard and the iron gate which opened onto the king's highway where they were safe. The key of David is the promise of victory in Christ over all that enslaves mankind. And this key is in each person's pocket.

CHAPTER 6

O Day-Spring

O Oriens. O Day-Spring, Brightness of Light everlasting, and Sun of Righteousness: Come and enlighten him that sitteth in darkness and the shadow of death.

O Come, thou Day-Spring, come and cheer
Our spirits by thine advent here;
Disperse the gloomy clouds of night,
And death's dark shadows put to flight:

For she [wisdom] is a reflection of eternal light (Wis 7:26).

But for you who fear my name the sun of righteousness shall rise, with healing in its wings (Mal 4:2).

Whereby the day-spring from on high has visited us, to give light to them that sit in darkness and in the shadow of death' (Lk 1:78, 79 *AV*. cf. Is. 9:2).

There can be few words of such universal significance as 'light'. It is both a common metaphor and a potent religious symbol. With its opposite, 'darkness', it is used to describe many a human condition. 'I am totally in the dark as to what he means, can you throw any light on the matter?' 'Light' and 'darkness' are among those archetypal symbols which the psychologist Jung wrote about as deeply imbedded in the collective unconscious of the human race and therefore formative of our basic attitudes to life and existence. So it is not surprising that the symbol of light is of great importance in many religions. One of the most beautiful prayers in the Hindu scriptures is 'Lead me from the unreal to the real, lead me from darkness to light, lead me from death to immortality' (*Brihadaranyaka Upanishad*), words which have been incorporated into the baptismal liturgy of the Church of South India. The Hindu festival of lights, *Diwali,*which, incidentally, usually falls quite close to Advent, celebrates the hope of returning light when the days are getting shorter. Muslims affirm 'God is the light of the heavens and earth' (Qur'an 24:35). The religion of ancient Persia, Zoroastrianism, calls God 'Ahura Mazda', Wise Lord and Lord of Light, and the sacred, ever burning fire symbolises the eternal divine light. The first specific thing which God created, according to the Genesis account, was light (Gen 1:3). It is interesting to note that the current 'Big Bang' theory about the origin of the universe begins with fundamental particles and radiation at extremely high temperature. To the ordinary person, this suggests something like a dense ball of light out of which the universe as we now know it condensed. At least that seems the only way to picture what happened.

The universal idea of light as closely related to God finds its fulfilment in the Jewish and Christian scriptures and preeminently in Christ, the light of the world. The Antiphon *O Oriens* is the one where the thought of Christ as light is uppermost, but this universal symbol is echoed in the others too. The book of Revelation describes the risen Christ as 'the root and offspring of David, the bright morning star' (22:16). The key of David frees us from the prison of 'darkness and the shadow of death'. Christ, divine wisdom, is 'a reflection of eternal light' (Wis 7:26) and the co-eternal Word of God is 'the true light that enlightens every man', which becomes wisdom incarnate (Jn 1:9).

'God is light' (1 Jn 1:5). When God acts to deliver his people from misfortune, his saving work is sometimes described as the coming of light, as in the familiar Christmas reading 'the people who walked in darkness have seen a great light' (Is 9:2). The darkness to which the prophet refers in his own day is the gloom of an Assyrian invasion and the light is God's action in saving his people from the cruel invader. These words, however, are rightly applied to the still greater act of salvation by which God saved his whole human family from a worse tyranny than that of Tiglath-Pileser or any earthly dictator, the bondage of sin, that all-pervading infection of our nature, a foreign body in God's good creation.

The light of God's saving action becomes identified with Christ because God's action is his presence in a unique way in the Word made flesh. St John describes the Word as 'the light of man' (1:4), 'the true light' (1:9). Similarly he records Christ as saying 'I am the light of the world; he who follows me will not walk in darkness but will have the light of life' (8:12). Christ referred to himself as the light of the world several times in John and this occasion was the feast of tabernacles, when 'four golden candlesticks were lit at night in the Court of Women (in the temple), and tradition had it that there was not a courtyard in Jerusalem that did not reflect the light' (*St John*, commentary by John Marsh, p.351). Christ is God's own light in the world by which he guides his people in the way of eternal life. The servant of God in Isaiah is described 'a light to the nations' (42:6, 49:6), words which Christians rightly apply to Christ along with Simeon in the *Nunc Dimittis* (Lk 2:32). Hebrews describes Christ as 'the brightness of (God's) glory' (1:3), following Wisdom 7:26. The longing for light, found among all peoples and supremely expressed in the Old Testament, is fulfilled in the coming of Christ the light into the world.

The antiphon brings out a special aspect of the light of Christ by its use of the word *Oriens*, rising sun, day-spring, dawn. It is new light, light after darkness, light which has conquered darkness. In some ways the most welcome light of all is the dawn which brings the long, weary night to an end. The psalmist finds in this figure a potent expression of the soul's longing for God: 'My soul waits for the LORD more than watchmen for the morning, more than watchmen for the morning' (130:6). It is not surprising that ancient peoples made the dawn a goddess, *Aurora* of the rosy fingers, called *Eos* by the Greeks and *Ushas* by the Hindus, who depict her as a beautiful maiden in crimson robes, golden veil, eternal but ever young.

The thought of God's light as the dawn is well captured in a poem in the latter part of Isaiah. 'Arise, shine; for your light has come, and the glory of the LORD has risen upon you' (Is 60:1). The prophet addresses Jerusalem, a city damaged and partly in ruins from invading armies, but destined for a glorious future. As the glow of dawn appears on the mountains and the rays of the rising sun light up the city streets, so God shines upon his people restoring them to his glory. 'The LORD will arise upon you, and his glory will be seen upon you. And nations shall come to your light, and kings to the brightness of your rising' (vv.2, 3). The light of God, reflected in the life of his people, will draw the nations to its radiance and cause them to praise God (v 6). The author speaks of the restored city in terms of wealth and magnificence and a temple as splendid as Solomon's. 'For the coastlands shall wait for me, the ships of Tarshish first, to bring your sons from far, their silver and gold with them' (v 9). 'The glory of Lebanon shall come to you, the cypress, the plane, the pine, to beautify the place of my sanctuary' (v 13). But he uses the imagery of gold, silver and cedar wood, making up the physical beauty of the temple, to inspire his hearers with the thought of God's recreation of them as a people glorious in their righteousness and obedience (v 21). His vision of the restoration of Jerusalem was never fully realised in historical fact; he seems to look beyond the physical splendour of the city to the transcendent reality of God's kingdom. 'The sun shall be no more your light by day, nor for brightness shall the moon give light to you by night; but the LORD will be your everlasting light, and your God will be your glory' (v 19). His words inspired the description of the heavenly city in Revelation where the 'glory of God is its light and its lamp is the lamb' (21:23). When we think of God coming to save us from a particular threat, we are naturally led on to think of the much greater glory yet to come. The extensive treatment of the themes of 'light' and the 'dawn' provided the Church with a rich supply of imagery to speak of the coming of Christ. Isaiah 60 is used specially in the liturgy of Epiphany, as well as in Advent and at Christmas. Its image of new light contributed to the antiphon *O Oriens*. There was another source for this word in the Vulgate version of Zechariah 3:8, 'For behold I will bring my servant the dawn' (*Orientem*) with which the composers of the antiphons would have been familiar. Modern versions, following the Hebrew, give the word 'branch' instead of dawn and that is undoubtedly the more accurate reading. This text relates more to the antiphon *O Radix Jesse*, the root or branch of Jesse, than to *O Oriens*, but they combine to deepen our understanding of the coming of our Redeemer.

The passage from Isaiah already referred to, 'The people who walked in darkness have seen a great light: those who dwelt in the land of deep darkness, on them the light has shined' (9:2), also conveys the thought of light as the dawn. The darkness of the people's captivity is lit up and banished by the dawning of the light of God's salvation. This verse is quoted in the Benedictus, appropriately a canticle of Morning Prayer, when Zechariah, father of the John who became the baptist, praises the God of Israel who has visited his people and set them free. He says 'the dawn from on high shall break upon us. To shine on those who dwell in darkness and the shadow of death: and to guide our feet into the way of peace' (Lk 1:78,79. *ICET text*). Isaiah's immediate reference was to the freedom of Israel from the Assyrians. His words are fulfilled in a much more wonderful way, as Zechariah proclaimed, by the coming of the Saviour, who gave 'his people knowledge of salvation by the forgiveness of all their sins' (*ibid* v 77). Jesus is the dawn which we long for above all things. He is the new light that fills us with hope, putting to flight the darkness of despair. The new light also guides us when we have been floundering in the darkness of ignorance, uncertainty and indecision by leading us into the way of peace, the wholeness of communion with God.

Dawn heralds a new day, and 'day' is another, related image frequent in the Advent theme. 'The night is far gone,' writes St Paul, 'the day is at hand' (Rom 13:12). He understood 'the day' as the time of Christ's appearance in glory, bringing human history to an end, and he assumed this would happen in the near future. Yet his use of the word has also a present reference. He urges his hearers, 'Let us then cast off the works of darkness and put on the armour of light; let us conduct ourselves becomingly as in the day' (vv 12,13). The 'day', obviously, is in some sense already come and that must be demonstrated in the lives of Christians. The same thought is found in his letter to the Thessalonians when he writes, 'For you are all sons of the light and of the day; we are not of the night or of darkness' (1 Thess 5,5) and 'Since we belong to the day, let us be sober, and put on the breastplate of faith and love, and for a helmet the hope of salvation' (v 8). 'The day of the Lord' is the future manifestation of God's glory throughout all his creation, which yet casts its light backwards to the present. It is now a glow of light in a dark world which gives promise of a greater glory to come. The thought of the new day brings together present and future so that our experience of Christ's dawning light fills us with hope for the glory of the noonday. 'The path of the righteous is like the light of dawn, which shines brighter and brighter until full day' (Prov 4:18).

The teaching of the New Testament encourages us to understand 'the righteous' as those who have been clothed with the righteousness of Christ, who have been enlightened by Christ, made partakers of his light, so that they shine with a reflected glow and can claim no glory for themselves in the good they do by God's grace. The enlightenment they enjoy is a foretaste of the full brightness of eternal glory and gives them a present experience of its fruition. 'Beloved, we are God's children now; it does not yet appear what we shall be, but we know that when he appears we shall be like him, for we shall see him as he is' (1 Jn 3:2).

The *Oriens*, the day-spring, is also described as 'the sun of right-eousness'. The phrase occurs in the prophet Malachi's exposition of the day of the Lord in which he warns the people of God's terri-ble judgement against evil. But this is not the main point of his teaching. God wishes no one to perish and makes provision for all to receive his mercy. 'But for you who fear my name, the sun of righteousness shall rise, with healing in its wings' (Mal 4:2). The fierce sun of lands in the latitude of Israel burns up the earth's plants, giving a striking metaphor for judgement. But God's judgement is the reverse side of his love which is poured out on everyone and its full extent is shown by contrast with the evil from which he frees us. The sun of righteousness is a burning de-structive flame to the evil in us, but a healing light bringing hope and joy to those who trust God's love and are open to his restor-ing power, just as the sun which destroys every struggling plant in desert areas can, under other circumstances, – the tropical rain forests – provide life, growth and health-giving energy to our planet.

'Righteousness' for the Hebrews had a strong sense of righting wrong, removing injustice and ensuring fair play to the poor, the weak and the disadvantaged in the community. The New Testa-ment in no way forgets this basic justice but adds the message of God's lavish, over-flowing gift of righteousness to those who, without any claim to deserve it, accept the gift at God's hands and become righteous through grace. In the prophet's thought 'the sun' is probably a figure for righteousness itself, but Christians can legitimately understand it as referring to Christ who brings this gift to the world. Christ came among us healing the sick, feed-ing the hungry, forgiving those weighed down by their sins, and by doing so is the bringer of life and health. The striking figure, 'with healing in its wings', has affinities with the religions of an-cient Babylonia and the surrounding countries where the sun god is depicted as a winged figure. In Greek mythology, Helios the sun god, drives a chariot across the heavens. He came to be identi-fied with Apollo who is God of healing. Malachi's image may have been borrowed from these sources but could also have arisen from simple observation of the daily journey of the sun from its rising to its setting. The psalmist can say 'If I take the wings of the morning and dwell in the uttermost parts of the sea' (i.e. the far-thest west) (139:9), to indicate the inescapable presence of God, using a figure suggested by the sun's movement across the sky from east to west. We noted a similar idea in Isaiah's picture of the dawn lighting up the ruined city of Jerusalem. As the rising sun lights up one point of earth after another in its onward journey, so the sun of righteousness shines over all, bringing healing and light.

Christ who has come, comes and is to come, is the light we long for as we pray 'Come and enlighten' us, *Veni et illumina*. Christ, who is himself the true light of the world, wishes to include us in the divine radiance and transform our nature, making us children of the light. St John's gospel contains the most references to Christ as the light of the world and he draws out the implications for Christ's followers: 'The light is with you for a little longer ... walk while you have the light ... believe in the light, that you may become sons of light'(12:35-6). 'I am the light of the world; he who follows me will not walk in darkness but will have the light of life' (8:12). There are a number of steps in our reception of Christ's light. The basic fact is Christ's nature as light, a light which shines in the world showing people where they are going, if they care to attend. At this stage they would be said to 'have' the light, but the further step, of 'I believe in the light' is necessary so that they may rely on it to direct their lives, and this leads on to the final step or, rather, life-long process, 'that you may become sons of light.' Christ attributed his own prerogative to his followers, when he said in the Sermon on the Mount, 'You are the light of the world.' The epistle to the Hebrews looks on the followers of Christ, the baptised, as those who were 'enlightened' (10:32) and Ephesians has the same thought: 'Once you were darkness, but now you are light in the Lord' (4:8). On the basis of what Christ has made us, these authors urge Christians to live accordingly. Christian ethics is the out-working of grace, the consequences in human behavi-our of what God has done in Christ for the human race, and of what he has made us through faith and sacraments. God, through baptism, has brought us into the kingdom of light and made us children of the light. The grace is available to the baptised to live out the consequences of their baptism in the tasks of everyday life. What we are by calling and grace, we need to become by daily obedience. One of the additional ceremonies of baptism in many traditions is the giving of a lighted candle to the newly baptised (or to their sponsors in the case of infants). The words accompanying this ceremony in the 1960 Indian Prayer Book are, 'Receive this light. This is to show that you have passed from darkness to light. Shine as a light in the world to the glory of God the Father.'

In baptism, the light of Christ is given to us; it is received by faith, the faith of the believing community as well as of the individual; we are incorporated into the community of faith, the company of the children of light; dwelling in the light of Christ which we have received in baptism, we are transformed by that light so that we become what our baptism declares us to be, the children of light.

In considering Christ the light, we have referred in passing to 'darkness and the shadow of death', but something more can be said about light's opposite. The conflict of light with darkness runs through the Bible, from the darkness on the face of the deep at the beginning of creation, which is dispersed by God's creative word 'Let there be light', to the final victory of light in the heavenly city – 'and there shall be no night there' (Rev 21:25). Isaiah's words of comfort and cheer show light as the deliverance of God's people from the gloom of darkness (9:2, 60:2). St John often describes Christ the light in contrast to darkness and its conqueror (1:54, 3:19, 8:12, etc). Where light is mentioned in the Bible, we generally find darkness as its opposite correlative. Yet it would be wrong to assume, with Zoroastrianism or any form of dualism, that the two are equal as well as opposite. Darkness is essentially negative – the absence of light. There are not two equal and opposite powers struggling for the mastery of all that is, with no certainty about the outcome. Good is the fundamental reality and evil, however powerful, all pervasive and destructive, is a corruption of good rather than a completely independent existence. The value of darkness as a metaphor of evil is that it brings out its essentially negative quality. It is misleading to say, without qualification, that evil is the absence of good. But if we fully assert the power and reality of evil in the world, we can affirm that the ultimate, strictly incomparable ground of everything is good. Satan, the prince of darkness, is not on a par with the God of all goodness as an equal and opposite power of evil. He is, in Christian tradition, an angel of light, a mighty potentate but subordinate to God who rebelled in his pride and can only corrupt and destroy but not create.

The battle between good and evil is none the less real, even though the final result is not in doubt. Evil is a powerful enemy which can only be defeated finally by God himself. Much of what Christ says about light is coupled with warnings against the strong and subtle force of darkness. Light pierces the disguises and tears off the masks which conceal evil and this sometimes produces dismay in the person who prefers to live in a world of comfortable illusion where he never has to face the evil in himself. 'For everyone who does evil hates the light, and does not come to the light, lest his deeds should be exposed' (Jn 3:20). We have a basic longing for the light and know that it is our only final happiness, but there is an initial resistance to the painful process of facing up to those elements of the truth about ourselves which are contrary to God's will. If anyone is finally lost, it will only be through persistent refusal of God's gift and rejection of his love, by allowing our nature to become so warped that, in Virgil's words, 'they cast their souls to hell through hate of light.'

Christ also warns us against postponing indefinitely our choice between light and darkness. 'The light is with you for a little longer. Walk while you have the light, lest the darkness overtake you' (Jn 12:35). The Advent note of urgency in our attitude to time is here sounded. The conflict between light and darkness is fought out in each human heart, and it is important to renew our allegiance daily to Christ the light. The Advent cry, 'Come, thou day-spring' is not only one of longing for the light, but also a plea for help to overcome the darkness within us and to aid the process of transformation of our nature into what we were made in baptism, children of light. A prayer in the night office of Compline uses the darkness of late evening as a metaphor for the sin against which we have a never-ending struggle: 'Illuminate the darkness of this night with thy celestial brightness, and from the sons of light banish the deeds of darkness.'

The phrase 'shadow of death' is a poetic parallel to 'darkness' (most evident in Is 9:2) which intensifies the idea. Modern versions usually translate it 'deep darkness' (though, as we shall see, there are many valuable associations attached to the more familiar phrase). It indicates the terror of the unknown as when Jeremiah speaks of the desert wanderings of the Israelites 'in a land that none passes through, where no one dwells' (Jer 2:6). The point Jeremiah makes is that God has protected his people from this great fear and brought them safely to a land of plenty, but they have forgotten his goodness. By reminding them of the 'deep darkness' of their wanderings, he highlights the gracious love of God. Similarly, Psalm 107 speaks of the gloom of captivity and of God's rescue: 'He brought them out of darkness and gloom, and broke their bonds asunder' (v 14).

The book of Job in several places speaks of deep darkness or gloom. When God faces Job with the great extent of his ignorance he asks him, 'Have you entered into the springs of the sea, or walked in the recesses of the deep? Have the gates of death been revealed to you, or have you seen the gates of deep darkness?' (38:16,17). In this passage, 'darkness' simply indicates the remote unknown (cf. 28:3). There is probably a similar usage in Job's passionate complaint to God against his sufferings when he pleads,'Let me alone that I may find a little comfort before I go whence I shall not return, to the land of gloom and deep darkness, the land of gloom and chaos, where light is as darkness' (10:20-22). Sheol, the abode of the dead, is a grey, remote world, akin to nothingness.

One passage, however, is a sustained impassioned protest about the enormity of the wicked under the metaphor of deep darkness. Job's point is that such people apparently prosper, while innocent men such as he suffer, but we are here concerned with how he uses the expression so effectively to portray evil:

There are those who rebel against the light,
who are not acquainted with its ways,
and do not stay in its paths.
The murderer rises in the dark,
that he may kill the poor and needy;
and in the night he is as a thief.
The eye of the adulterer also waits for the twilight, saying, 'No eye will see me';
In the dark they dig through houses;
by day they shut themselves up;
they do not know the light.
For deep darkness is morning to all of them;
for they are friends with the terrors of deep darkness.
(Job 24:13-17)

This is rampant, self-chosen, defiant evil like the people of whom our Lord said 'They loved darkness rather than light.'

Apart from Job, most of the passages which speak of 'deep darkness' treat it as a contrast to the freedom and joy which God gives. It is a stage from which people turn in grateful relief to the Lord of light, a dark prison house which God enters to rescue them and lead them into the bright realm of communion with him. This point is perhaps made more clearly in the Authorised Version, which renders the phrase in all the texts quoted as 'the shadow of death', an expression dear to many from its associations with Psalm 23:4, 'Yea, though I walk through the valley of the shadow of death, I will fear no evil: for thou art with me; thy rod and thy staff they comfort me' (AV). 'The shadow of death' can refer literally to a time of dying or bereavement, or metaphorically to any experience of depression, fear or despair. To articulate one's anxiety or sorrow is to be helped work through it, and we are led on to emphasise the joy God's presence brings to the lonely and depressed, just as a sunny day coming after a period of cloud and rain lifts one's spirits all the more. The coming of the Lord is essentially the irruption of eternal joy into the grey drabness of a life without God, as all the antiphons, and particularly *O Oriens*, testify. The hymn based on them with, the repeated 'Rejoice' in the chorus, accentuates the cheerful nature of what Advent means. Christ is the 'cheering light' invoked in the ancient Greek hymn, *Phos Hilarion*.

A perhaps accidental thought in the word 'shadow' is worth noting. Light causes shadow only in the sense that it illuminates the area round the place where something blocks the light from shining. People create their own darkness by putting up walls against the light. The struggle against darkness can be intense and only God is strong enough to rescue us from its power, yet the darkness of evil is essentially our own choice which results from our rejection of God and shutting ourselves off from his light and life. As Christian, in Doubting Castle, had the key in his pocket to unlock his prison doors, so everyone can escape from the prison of darkness and the shadow of death by turning to the light of Christ.

CHAPTER 7

O King of the Nations

O Rex Gentium. O King of the nations, and their Desire; the Corner-stone who makest both one: Come and save mankind, whom thou formedst of clay.

O Come, Desire of nations! show
Thy kingly reign on earth below;
Thou Corner-stone, uniting all,
Restore the ruin of our fall.

Just and true are thy ways O King of the ages (var. nations) ... (Rev 15:3),

The desire of all nations shall come (Hag 2:7 *AV*).

Christ Jesus himself being the corner-stone (Eph 2:20).

For he is our peace who has made us both one (Eph 2:14).

The LORD God formed man of dust from the ground (Gen 2:7).

Monarchy has been abolished in many countries in this century, whether through violent revolution or peaceful evolution of new forms of government. Yet kings, queens and the members of royal families have a peculiar fascination for many people, not least in those countries which no longer have them. A coronation or a royal wedding will command on television a viewing public of millions. The person and office of a king has a mystique and an aura which strikes a chord in our consciousness and conveys a unique sense of honour, devotion and loyalty.

It is understandable,therefore, that we should use language borrowed from royal pageantry to express our allegiance to God and attempt to convey something of his greatness. No other term but 'king' will do as a metaphor for this particular aspect of God's nature. He is 'the king of glory', 'King of kings and Lord of lords', the Lord upon the throne 'crowned with many crowns', 'the king eternal'. Try substituting any other term drawn from modern democratic politics and the result is ludicrous. It is interesting and reassuring to note that, in the recent flowering of new hymns and charismatic songs, words like 'king' and 'reign' are still found.

Quite rightly, we limit the power of our rulers because we know from history that no human being can be trusted with absolute power. For the sake of public order and the protection of individuals and society, we delegate certain powers to groups of people who, in democratic countries, govern us with our consent, but we have checks and balances to ensure that the power entrusted to them is not abused. That is why the vocabulary of modern politics cannot provide terms for the worship of God, because he does not rule us with delegated authority but by absolute right. Though most kings and queens in today's world are constitutional monarchs and have less actual power than the elected rulers, yet the symbols of royalty are more suitable to show the absolute, unconditional allegiance we owe to God than any democratic concept because they point to an authority over and beyond ourselves.

The antiphon 'O King of the nations' adds this highly evocative term for God to the others we have been considering, in order to articulate the Advent longing for the coming of the Lord with power and authority, in just and kindly rule, into the chaos and misery of a disordered world. Both God and Christ are frequently described as 'king' in the Bible, though the actual phrase 'king of the nations' only occurs as a variant reading to 'king of the ages' in Rev 15:3.

Often the term 'king' is used for pure adoration of God and Christ, particularly by the Psalms in the Old Testament and the book of Revelation in the New. 'The LORD of hosts, he is the King of glory!' (Ps 24:10). 'The LORD sits enthroned as king for ever' (Ps 29:10). These are typical of the many verses in the Psalms where God is adored as king. The prophet Isaiah also finds the language of kingship suitable for speaking of God. In the well-known passage where he describes his vision of God and call to be a prophet, he says 'my eyes have seen the King , the Lord of hosts' (Is 6:5). The whole passage breathes awe, adoration and self-abasement before the majesty of God. We also find in a later passage longing for God and for the protection he gives his people: 'Your eyes will see the king in his beauty ... For the LORD is our judge, the LORD is our ruler, the LORD is our king; he will save us' (33:17,22).

When God is described as king in the Old Testament, the meaning often is 'king of Israel', as is sometimes explicitly stated (Is 44:6, Zeph3:15). Following in this tradition, Nathaniel says to Christ, 'Rabbi ... You are the King of Israel!' (Jn 1:49). But even the Old Testament by no means limits God's kingship to the chosen people. Psalm 2 speaks of the king reigning in Zion as ruler of all the kings of the earth. Psalm 93 describes God as reigning over nature - the floods, the waves of the sea – and Psalm 96 describes him as universal ruler and judge: 'Say among the nations "the LORD reigns ... he will judge the people with equity"'(v 10). The prophet Zechariah explicitly declared that in the day of the Lord's coming, 'The LORD will become king over all the earth' (14:9).

Christ, as God's Son, is likewise king both of Israel and of the whole world. The Messiah, the anointed one, is a royal title, a new

King David. Though Christ was reluctant to accept the title 'king' in the days of his flesh, because of the obvious political misunderstanding which it would provoke, Christian devotion, beginning in the New Testament,finds the language of kingship specially appropriate in which to praise and worship him. The bulk of his recorded teaching was about the kingdom of God and in the light of his resurrection it was natural for his followers to hail him as, with God, the king of that kingdom.

St Paul sees him as a warrior king engaged in the subjugation of enemies throughout all created realms: 'For he must reign until he has put all his enemies under his feet' (1 Cor 15:25). In the words of Revelation, 'The kingdom of the world has become the kingdom of our Lord and of his Christ and he shall reign for ever and ever' (11:15).

Revelation is especially the book of Christ the King. The author, John, living as a prisoner on Patmos under the cruel rule of the Roman emperor Domitian, takes courage from the almighty eternal rule of the ascended Christ, the Lamb who was slain, seated at God's right hand, and encourages the persecuted Churches in Asia Minor to find their strength in the same Christ who will conquer those who make war on him, 'for he is Lord of Lords and King of kings, and those with him are called and chosen and faithful' (Rev 17:14). Christ is portrayed as sharing in this universal Lordship and receives worship with God from every people and nation. 'And I heard every creature in heaven and on earth and under the earth and in the sea and all therein saying, "To him who sits upon the throne and to the Lamb be blessing and honour and glory and might for ever and ever!"'(5:13).

'King' and 'Lord' often go together, both in ordinary speech and in the Bible, as many of the above quotations show. The earliest Christian Creed is probably 'Jesus is Lord' (1 Cor 12:3). We find here a valuable link with the antiphon *O Adonai*. The king of the nations is the Lord God, the Lord Jesus Christ, 'The LORD' as a reverent expression of the Divine name, too holy to utter, of the God of Israel. The terms 'King' and 'Lord' reinforce each other as we use them to adore our God and his Christ and beseech him to come and deliver us.

Another link with *O Adonai* is provided through the idea of the shepherd-king, which we touched on in relation to the phrase 'leader of the house of Israel'. It was customary in Israel and the surrounding countries to describe kings as 'shepherds'. David himself was literally a shepherd of his father's flocks before he became a soldier of Saul and later replaced him as king. The prophets often criticise Israel's rulers as faithless shepherds who exploit and despoil the sheep instead of feeding them. Ezekiel has a long diatribe against unworthy shepherds and, as a remedy, hears God's words 'I myself will be the shepherd of my sheep' (34:15). He goes on to state that God will shepherd his people through an ideal king: 'And I will set over them one shepherd, my servant David, and he shall feed them: he shall feed them and be their shepherd. And I, the LORD will be their God, and my servant David shall be prince among them' (vv 23, 24).

Ezekiel probably envisaged a new and faithful king of the Davidic dynasty who would govern his people justly, free from foreign rule. His words were fulfilled in a much more wonderful way by the coming of the Messiah, the shepherd-king who gave his life for the sheep and who rose again to be the great shepherd and guardian of our souls.

In spite of the great value of the term 'king' to evoke God's glory and majesty and the absolute allegiance we owe to him, it is still a human analogy with all the limitations that implies. We can retain the advantages of the term without its defects if we determine its meaning by God's rule, rather than the other way round, interpreting God's kingship by human monarchs. Christ transformed the titles which have been given to him and the terms of Jewish expectation, particularly that of 'Messiah' itself. In the same way, he greatly alters our human ideas of 'king', sometimes to the point of turning them upside down. From one point of view, it is surprising that the Bible should use the word 'king' to describe God and Christ in view of the deplorable examples of kings found in its pages. Yet Christ gave the bulk of his teaching in terms of the kingdom of God, although there was no king in Israel when he taught and the previous king was the ruthless tyrant Herod.

The Bible as a whole is ambivalent in its attitude to kings. The Old Testament authors differ in their views about the kings of Israel. The author of Judges, viewing them in an idealistic light, explains some particularly deplorable episodes in the nation's life by saying 'In those days there was no king in Israel; every man did what was right in his own eyes' (17:6. 18:1, etc). 1 Samuel records the institution of the monarchy as a concession to the people's demands (ch 8) which though permitted and ordained by God is, in one sense, a rejection of God's kingly rule. Samuel addressed the people: 'You said to me. "No, but a king shall reign over us," when the LORD your God was your king. And now behold the king whom you have chosen, for whom you have asked; behold, the LORD has set a king over you' (1 Sam 12:12,13).

Samuel anointed Saul as Israel's first king and later appointed David in the same way, so that the king is described as 'the LORD'S anointed'. The Hebrew word for 'anointed' is the basis of the title 'Messiah', of which the Greek equivalent is 'Christ'. The messianic Psalm 2 states 'The kings of the earth set themselves against the LORD and against his anointed' (v 2) and gives God's answer to their futile opposition, 'I have set my king on Zion, my holy hill' (v 6). As David was regarded as the nearest to Israel's ideal king (though the flaws in his character are plainly recorded) so the Messiah is regarded as another David, or the son of David. The prophets speak of David as king in the future (eg. Jer 30:9) and this provided a terminology sometimes used of Jesus in the gospels (eg. Mk 10:47).

The gospel writers, with some degree of hindsight, describe the whole life of Jesus as that of a king. Matthew tells of the eastern astrologers who, at his birth, come seeking the 'king of the Jews' (2:2). We have already noted how, according to St John, Nathaniel hailed him at the beginning of his ministry as 'the King of Israel'. Jesus himself does not reject the title, though it is often given with misunderstanding and sometimes with malice, as when the chief priests accuse him to Pilate of claiming to be king of the Jews in order to have him convicted of sedition (Lk23:2). After the feeding of the five thousand, in John's version, the people were about to 'take him by force and make him king' (Jn 6:15) but Jesus slipped away from them, no doubt because the time was not right and because their idea of kingship was so different from his own. Yet he deliberately rode into Jerusalem on a donkey in full awareness of Zechariah's words (9:9) 'Lo, your king comes to you; triumphant and victorious is he, humble and riding on an ass.' He accepted the Hosannas of the people, their actions in spreading the road before him with palms and garments, and defended his disciples when criticised by the Pharisees for saying 'Blessed is the King who comes in the name of the Lord!' (Lk 19:38-40).

The nature of Christ's kingship is a dominant theme in St John's account of his trial before Pilate. Again, Jesus does not deny that he is a king but insists 'My kingship is not of this world' (18:36). There is tragic irony in the intrigues of the Jewish priests to have Jesus condemned as a threat to Caesar's rule, and Pilate's vacillating attempts to acquit him because he sees through their intrigues but hadn't the courage to act on his knowledge, when all the time Jesus is not a rival king to Caesar but immeasurably greater, King of kings and Lord of lords. The Roman soldiers hail Jesus as a king only to mock him. At the crucifixion, bystanders taunt him as the king who can't come down from the cross and his name and 'crime' written on the cross are 'Jesus of Nazareth, King of the Jews'. In all these cases, the words used in mockery are true in a sense undreamed of by the people who spoke or wrote them. Christ, by his sacrificial death for the world and his rising again as Lord of all, defines what kind of king he is. The antiphon, 'O Root of Jesse', contains the words 'at whom kings shall shut their mouths; curl their lips in disgust.' The one whom ordinary kings despise is the true king.

'He saved others; he cannot save himself. Let the Christ, the King of Israel, come down from the cross' (Mk 15:31,32). All of these mocking words are profoundly true. It is ironic that Christ's mockers should connect his kingship with his saving role. One of the functions of a king in ancient times was to be a powerful warrior who would lead his armies into battle and defend his country from the enemy. When the Israelites first asked Samuel for a king and he tried to dissuade them, they replied 'No! but we will have a king over us, that we also may be like all the nations, and that our king may govern us and go out before us and fight our battles' (1 Sam 8:19,20). We pray in the antiphon 'O king of the nations ... come and save mankind.' We look to our king to be our saviour. A warrior king, who drove back the enemy and saved his country from invasion, would also save himself and his throne. But Christ's mockers spoke more truly than they knew when they said 'He saved others; he cannot save himself.' Only by not saving himself could he save others. His rule over creation and his defeat of evil were accomplished by rejecting force, refusing to let his servants fight (Jn 18:36) and allowing himself to become the victim of the hate and cruelty which make up the sin of man's rebellion against God.

Ancient peoples looked to their kings not only to protect them from their enemies outside their countries - the foreign invaders – but also to govern them wisely and justly, settling disputes and protecting the poor and weak against the rich and powerful. Solomon was even asked to adjudicate who was the mother of a disputed child (1 Kgs 3:16-28). Hence wisdom was a quality much to be desired in kings. Wisdom, personified in the book of Proverbs, says 'By me kings reign, and rulers decree what is just' (8 :15). The antiphons 'O Wisdom' and 'O King of the nations' are interrelated in this respect and together express our longing for God to bring stability and wise ordering to the problems of peace, justice and fair shares for all in the complex world in which we live.

The word 'king' emphasises the inequality between us and God. He has absolute authority over us and demands our unconditional obedience. It comes as a surprise, therefore, to find that the Bible depicts the divine kingship as shared with human beings. There may be a hint of this in the Old Testament phrase 'kingdom of priests' (Ex 19:6) but it is explicitly stated in many parts of the New Testament. An early Christian hymn states 'If we endure, we shall also reign with him' (2 Tim 2:12). Amid the rebukes to the church in Laodicea, which was neither cold nor hot, we find the promise 'He who conquers, I will grant him to sit with me on my throne' (Rev 3:21). The company of heaven praises the Lamb with the words 'Thou wast slain and by thy blood didst ransom men for God from every tribe and tongue and people and nation, and hast made them a kingdom and priests to our God, and they shall reign on earth' (Rev 5:9,10).

Human kings are often jealous of their power because they think that if it is shared with others they will grow weaker. But God delights to share not only his kingship but his holiness and even his divine nature with us human beings. God is self-giving love, who in creation shares the gift of existence with things other than himself and by his incarnation brought us into special relationship with himself. Christ is God's unique Son, yet he is called our brother (Rom 8:29) because God has adopted us as his children. Christ is the world's true light, yet in him we can shine as lights to the world. He is the true vine, but makes us his branches. He is our great high priest, but those who believe in him are 'a royal priesthood'. In the same way, the King of kings and Lord of lords makes us kings too. 'Christ is King, surely, but he is not a king whose royalty is diminished by sharing it with other people' (Geoffrey Preston, *Hallowing the Time*, p.41).

It is essential to remember the kind of king Christ is when we speak of sharing in his kingship. The natural tendency of fallen men is to lord it over their fellows when they get the chance. Democracy is an attempt to curb the domination of the strong over the weak by stressing equal rights for all, e.g. by the right of all to vote. This inevitably means a 'levelling down' of people. The kingdom of God is a divine gift to the human race, offered for our acceptance by faith, which 'levels up' its members by a share in Christ's kingly rule. But this offer can only be received by the meek, the child-like and those who take to heart our Lord's teaching that the greatest among his disciples must become as the one who serves (Lk 22:25-30). When we pray 'Come, O King of the nations' in the right spirit our Lord, amazingly, answers our prayer by letting us reign with him in his kingdom.

'O king of the nations and their desire ...' So far we have referred incidentally to the longing of people for God's reign on earth. This is a theme running through much of the Bible, although the actual phrase 'their desire', *desideratus earum* (Hag.2:7) in the Vulgate, followed by the Authorised Version, is probably a misunderstanding of the original. The prophet Haggai urged the people of Jerusalem after the return from exile to rebuild the temple and proclaimed to them God's promise 'I will shake all nations, so that the *treasures* ('desire', *AV*) of all nations shall come in, and I will fill this house with splendour, says the LORD of hosts' (*ibid*). The thought is that God will gather the precious materials, gold, silver and fine wood, 'desirable things' from far and wide to beautify his temple. Yet 'desire of nations', in the sense of what the world yearns for, is a phrase with long associations of devotion and is amply justified by the Bible as a whole and many explicit texts. It is only necessary to note that even in the Old Testament this desire for God's rule is found among the Gentiles as well as the chosen people. We have already seen that the Root of Jesse stands as 'an ensign to the peoples; him shall the nations seek' (ch 4 above). The prophet Zechariah attributes to the Gentiles also the longing for God so often found on the lips of Israel. 'Many peoples and strong nations shall come to seek the LORD of hosts in Jerusalem, and to entreat the favour of the LORD' (8:22. See the whole paragraph, vv 20-23).

There is no need to show from the New Testament the widespread desire of the world's peoples for the kingdom of God. One example can represent all, the Greeks who came to the apostle Philip and said 'Sir, we wish to see Jesus' (Jn 12:21). The dialogue following this request includes the words 'I, when I am lifted up from the earth, will draw all men to myself' (v 32).

'O King of the nations, and their Desire ... Come and save mankind.' The prayer of the antiphon is the same as the petition in the Lord's Prayer, 'Thy kingdom come, thy will be done, in earth as it is in heaven.' The coming of the kingdom is the coming of the king to establish his rule on earth and bring all things into subjection to his holy and loving will. This is what the human race yearns for, even if its deepest desire is hidden under the distractions and pressures of a restless age.

One of the functions of a king is to be a symbol of national unity, a thought further developed in the phrase 'the Corner-stone who makest both one'. In modern states the constitutional monarch can be quite a powerful symbol, while in ancient times he was expected to be judge and leader and army commander as well so that he might be a strong bond to hold his people together. Isaiah described princes as the 'cornerstones' for their tribes (19:13), though in the particular case he mentions they did not live up to their people's expectations.

The early Christians had two favourite proof-texts about corner-stones from the Old Testament in their controversies with the Jews. The use of one of them, 'the stone which the builders rejected has become the head of the corner' (Ps 118:22) goes back to our Lord's parable of the wicked tenant-farmers (Mk 12:1-11, quoted in v 10). But the other text is more directly relevant to the antiphon: 'Thus says the Lord GOD, "Behold I am laying in Zion for a foundation a stone, a tested stone, a precious cornerstone, of a sure foundation"' (Is 28:16). This saying would appear to be the basis of the phrase in Ephesians, 'Christ Jesus himself being the cornerstone' (2:20). The whole passage, vv 14-22, lies behind the words of the antiphon, 'the Corner-stone who makest both one,' as it is a celebration of the unity which Christ brings and the gospel proclaims. The word 'both' refers to Jew and Gentile whom Christ has reconciled to God and to each other by his cross. One of the greatest divisions in the ancient world was that between Jew and Gentile and, in overcoming that division by the sacrifice of himself, Christ destroyed, in principle, all the barriers which keep people apart.

The saving work of Christ can be described in terms of unity, as the epistle to the Ephesians does. It presents God's eternal purpose as 'to unite all things in Christ' (1:10). The word translated 'unite' means literally 'to bring again under one head'. The underlying thought is that the original unity of creation under God's headship, which has been marred and broken by evil, is restored again in Christ. St Paul sees the cross as a cosmic act which defeats the supernatural powers of evil and brings the whole spiritual and material universe into a unity again (eg. Col 1:20). The reconciliation of sinful human beings to God is set in this cosmic framework. God's will, the coming of his kingdom, is the restoration of universal harmony under his sovereign rule.

The figure of 'the cornerstone' is particularly apt to describe Christ's role of reconciliation. The cornerstone is the place where two walls of a building at right angles to each other meet, and as such has a key function in holding the building together. Both St Paul and St Peter describe Christians as forming a building of living stones held together by Christ and (with some mixing of metaphors) growing up to maturity in him so that they may be a fit dwelling place for God through his Spirit (Eph 2:19-22; 1 Pet 2:4-5). A world torn apart by conflicts based on colour, race, religion, inequality of wealth and many other causes, desperately needs the unifying power of Christ. In Christ differences need not be abolished, though injustice must be removed, but they can be combined into a rich and living unity. In that spirit, we pray to Christ, the cornerstone who binds us together, to come and deliver us from sin which separates us from God and each other.

The final words of the antiphon, 'whom thou formedst of clay', have profound and subtle links with those which go before and beautifully round off this prayer to God. They refer to God's creation of the human race, 'then the LORD God formed man of dust from the ground' (Gen 2:7). The reference is even clearer when we compare the Latin of the antiphon, *quem de limo formasti*, with the verse in the Vulgate, *Formavit igitur Dominus Deus hominem de limo terrae*.

The 'clay' of our common humanity takes up and reinforces the thought of the universal reconciliation achieved by Christ the King. We are fully part of the material universe and Christ's redeeming work does not cut us off from our earthly roots but is part of his gathering up of all things in one. Today, when human mastery over nature has advanced so far that we are in danger of destroying our planet, we can see more clearly the connection between human sin and the pollution of the environment, 'cursed is the ground because of you' (Gen 3:17). We can also see that redemption of human beings from sin has repercussions on the earth, which is our home, and understand a little of what St Paul means by his mysterious words 'the creation itself will be set free from its bondage to decay and obtain the glorious liberty of the children of God' (Rom 8:21).

By reminding us that we are formed of clay, the antiphon keeps us humble and drives away a false spirituality which despises the body and seeks to escape from it like the Gnostic heretics in the early Church. 'Come and save mankind whom thou formedst of clay.' We do not ask God to save us from our bodies, but that we may glorify him in our bodies, rejoicing in our kinship with the animal world and the whole physical universe. The glory of the gospel is that God should delight to enter into fellowship with us creatures of earthly flesh who are 'like the beasts that perish'. The whole of our being is God's creation and though our physical nature is constantly changing and decaying, it has some relationship with eternal life. The doctrine of the resurrection of the body has often been taught in crudely physical ways, which has probably caused many modern people to reject it. But, correctly understood, it asserts the significance of the whole of our nature, all we are and do, in God's gift to us of eternal life. It is not that a small part of us will survive death but that God will transform and recreate the whole person and, in that state, there will be something analogous to our present bodies, unimaginably altered.

Our creation from 'clay', the dust of the earth, is set in the Genesis story of God making one man, Adam, which teaches the essential unity of the human race. This story, which is not historical fact, conveys the truth in a way nothing else can. We are all of one blood, related to each other in the family of man. All human divisions are quarrels within one family and our Advent prayer to Christ is that he will come and unite us in himself, the second Adam.

We were created in God's image and likeness (Gen 1:26-27) but sin has marred and defaced that image. Christ came to restore us, not simply to a state of Paradisal innocence, but to a more wonderful condition where sin is forgiven and evil conquered through our union with God made man in Jesus Christ. St Paul expounds the parallelism between the two states in his teaching on the resurrection of the dead, when the result of Christ's salvation is fully worked out. 'Just as we have borne the image of the man of dust,' God's image disfigured by sin, 'we shall also bear the image of the man of heaven,' a new and more wonderful creation by the divine gift of Christ (1 Cor 15:49). An ancient collect, restored in some modern Prayer Books for the Sunday after Christmas, expresses the same thought.

> Almighty God, who wonderfully created us in your own image, and yet more wonderfully restored us through your Son Jesus Christ: grant that as he came to share in our humanity, so we may share the life of his divinity.

The antiphon is the cry of humanity, in its earthly state yet longing for union with the divine, to be remade in God's image and reunited through Christ, the king of the universe, with its source in God. 'Come and save mankind whom thou formedst of clay.'

CHAPTER 8

O Emmanuel

O Emmanuel, our King and Lawgiver, the Desire of all nations, and their Salvation: Come and save us, O Lord our God.

O Come, O come, Emmanuel,
And ransom captive Israel,
That mourns in lonely exile here,
Until the Son of God appear.

His name shall be called Emmanuel (which means God with us) (Mt 1:23, cf Is 7:14).

For the creation waits with eager longing for the revealing of the sons of God (Rom 8:19).

O Emmanuel is the climax of the Great'O's. It is appointed for the day before Christmas Eve when we are about to celebrate the coming of God to earth in human flesh. St Matthew translates the Hebrew word, 'God with us', for his Greek-speaking readers. In this antiphon we celebrate the presence of God and confidently ask him to save us because we know he has come among us. On any reckoning, *O Emmanuel* is the greatest and most important of the antiphons, which is rightly given a prominent place as the culmination of them all. The hymn based on the antiphons makes it equally prominent by putting it at the beginning.

Since it is the last and climax of the antiphons, *O Emmanuel* repeats phrases and ideas which have occurred previously, in particular 'king' and 'lawgiver'. These two words are significant as they indicate the great difference between us and God, the vast gap between creator and creature, ruler and ruled. 'Lawgiver' occurs in the other antiphon with a Hebrew title, *O Adonai*, which means 'Lord' and is also a reverent way of indicating, without uttering, the divine name. The astounding truth conveyed by the name 'Emmanuel' is that Almighty God has made his home with us but, in order to appreciate that truth, we need to emphasise the transcendent, divine nature of the one who so humbled himself. In the same way, it was only after we had drawn out of the term 'king' the sense of awe and majesty and distance above us which it implies that we were able to accept the wonder of Christ's gift that we should reign as kings with him. Emmanuel is our divine king who commands our obedience to his laws by absolute right. In asking him to come and save us, we address him as 'O Lord our God'.

The original context of the word 'Emmanuel' is in the prophecy of Isaiah. As with many other words and concepts which Christians used to described Christ's coming, it was coined in a time of threatened invasion. Ahaz, king of Judah, was under military pressure to join Israel and Syria in a coalition to resist the might of Assyria. Isaiah received a message from God to strengthen the resolve of the vacillating and unreliable king. He said that a young woman would bear a child and name him Emmanuel (Is 7:14). Isaiah said that, before the child was old enough to tell the difference between good and evil, the armed threat against Judah would be removed. In fact, a worse evil will come to it – an Assyrian invasion (v 17).

It is clear that Isaiah is primarily referring to events in the near future for his country. The two kings of Syria and Israel, who are at present threatening Judah, will be defeated before the child named Emmanuel is grown up, hence the birth of the child is imminent. The child's identity is hotly disputed and commentators also disagree about whether Isaiah proclaimed a time of peace and prosperity or gloom and doom, or (as seems most likely) one followed by the other. Fortunately in our study of 'Emmanuel' as an Advent title, we do not have to decide on these difficult questions. The immediate reference of Isaiah's words is to the activity of God in relation to his people when they were in danger and perplexity, an activity which included rescue from foreign invasion, at least in the short term. God is with his people in the sense that he has come to their aid when they are assailed by their foes. If there is also the sense that God is with them in judgement, that the sin and folly of the nation bring national disaster, then we have the salutary lesson that God's presence is not something we can use purely for our own ends, but condemns our self-chosen, evil ways and is a call to bring our lives under his rule.

The meaning of Isaiah's words is not exhausted by their immediate reference to the political events towards the end of the eighth century BC. St Matthew, followed by universal Christian tradition, sees in them the promise of a much more wonderful presence of God with us in the birth of our Saviour. It will be our task to draw out the full meaning, as far as we can, of 'Emmanuel' as indicating the presence of Christ in his incarnation, continuing communion with us and final appearing. But before considering the New Testament interpretation of the title, it is necessary to look at how the concept of 'God with us' is used in the Bible as a whole.

The word 'Emmanuel' only occurs three times in the Bible, in Is 7:14, 8:8 and Mt 1:23, but the idea it expresses is found in practically every book, if not chapter. The Bible portrays God in active, dynamic terms rather than as a metaphysical concept. So the basic meaning of 'God with us' is that God acts on our behalf. This meaning is well illustrated in the dialogue of Gideon with God, or God's angel, in the time of the Judges when Israel was overrun by the Midianites. God's angel greeted Gideon: 'The LORD is with you, you mighty man of valour' (Jgs 6:12). Gideon replied: 'If the LORD is with us, why has this befallen us?. The Lord has cast us off and given us into the hand of Midian' (v 13). God reassures him, 'I will be with you, and you shall smite the Midianites as one man' (v 16).

In many cases, 'God with us' means that God does something to save us from some predicament. Psalm 46 has the refrain 'The LORD of hosts is with us, the God of Jacob is our refuge' (vv 7,11) which is well explained in the first verse: 'God is ... a very present help in trouble.' This sense of 'God with us' perfectly fits the circumstances when the name 'Emmanuel' was first given. God was 'with' the people of Judah in that he rescued them from the armed might of their neighbours Israel and Syria. The meaning of the phrase is closely akin to 'for us' or 'on our side', when St Paul writes 'If God is for us, who is against us?'(Rom 8:13).

Nowadays we rightly feel hesitant to claim that God is on our side when we think of the number of times in the past opposing countries in war have both prayed for victory to the same God. We can only make the claim safely if we submit to God's loving will for the good of all and pray that our desires may be conformed to his. Isaiah's promise to Ahaz was by no means that God gave unconditional support to Judah but was a message of judgement and a call to obedience as well as a promise of help.

The hymn verse relating to 'O Emmanuel' speaks of 'captive Israel' and its 'lonely exile'. In doing so it goes beyond the words of the antiphon, but it is a fitting allusion to the threat of captivity and exile in the word's original context, though it understands these concepts symbolically. 'Exile' refers to the absence of the Messiah, a state of being bereft of God's presence, and longing for the Messiah to rescue Israel from that state by the coming of God's own Son.

The phrase, or idea, of 'God with us' is by no means confined to situations of calamity or danger. It often signifies the fullness of blessing which God's presence brings. God promised Joshua, when he succeeded Moses as leader of the Israelites, 'as I was with Moses, so I will be with you; I will not fail you or forsake you' (Josh 1:5). When Boaz goes to his fields at harvest time, he greets his reapers 'The LORD be with you,' and they reply 'The LORD bless you' (Ruth 2:4). On similar occasions in rural Ireland one hears 'God bless the work!' The greeting in the Christian liturgy is in the identical words of Boaz. As we worship together, we wish each other the fullness of God's blessing.

It would be impossible to look at every place in the Bible where the idea of 'God with us' is found, and there is no need to do so. The Advent cry 'O Emmanuel' relates especially to 'God with us' in the fully human person of Jesus Christ, born on this earth in the reign of the Roman Emperor Augustus and with us always till his final appearance in glory. St Matthew says that Christ's birth 'fulfilled' Isaiah's prophecy of Emmanuel. We cannot understand this as meaning that Isaiah simply predicted an event which took place over seven hundred years later, not least because Isaiah had a message for his countrymen in their own period of time. Yet Isaiah's words bear a meaning which goes beyond their immediate reference and proclaims God's continuing presence with his people, leading to the wonder of his incarnate presence. In the next chapter, Isaiah speaks of the more fearful Assyrian threat after the danger from Syria and Israel has passed. He uses the figures of a great bird of prey for the Assyrian army and states, 'its outspread wings will fill the breadth of your land, O Immanuel' (Is 8:8). Some commentators argue, surely correctly, that Emmanuel here is the ruler of the land, not merely a name given to a child to mark a contemporary event. This is one step in the process leading to the identification of Emmanuel with the expected Messiah. It is reinforced by the statement in the following chapter, 'to us a child is born', who will be 'Prince of Peace' (9:6), and Micah's reference to the birth of a child who is to be ruler (5:2-4).

In the following centuries, as the country experienced repeated invasion and deliverance, the longing for God's special intervention to save his people grew into the concept of the Messiah, as understood by the Jews just before and during the lifetime of Jesus. When Matthew says the birth of Christ 'fulfilled' the prophecy of Isaiah, we can understand this (whatever may have been the evangelist's own ideas) as indicating the link between God's gracious care for his people in the past and the climax of that care in the incarnation of his Son. Christ did not come to earth as an afterthought on God's part, but in fulfilment of his eternal plan to save mankind. Christians understand the history of Israel and the Jews as leading up to, and preparing his people for, the coming of his Son in human flesh. Christ's coming is promised and foreshadowed in the Old Testament, but when he came he far surpassed the promise and expectation of the people. He was the Messiah of the Jews, but he won no military victories or political power, and suffered the fate, unimagined for a Messiah, of death by crucifixion. On the other hand, as his followers reflected on his nature, they came to see that he was on a level with God, to be worshipped and adored with God the Father. The title 'Emmanuel' took on a much deeper and fuller meaning than it has in the context of Isaiah's prophecy. God is not only with us, in the sense of acting on our behalf to save us from our enemies, but has become flesh and dwelt among us.

Christ was a man living with other men and women as one of themselves on this earth for about thirty three years. He grew up in a carpenter's family, no doubt played with the children around him, attended the synagogue, was taught the Scriptures with other pupils and, when he reached the age of about thirty, was baptised by John with other penitents. He rejected no one who came to him for healing or relief from genuine need. Unlike the religious leaders of his day, he had a special affinity with society's rejects, the hated tax-collectors and loose women, who were strangely drawn to him and whose society he was pleased to share. He chose a group of twelve ordinary men, four of them fishermen, whom he taught and prepared for a future without his physical presence and commanded them to break bread and drink wine as his memorial with the mysterious words 'This is my body', 'This is my blood'. He was crucified, not alone, but alongside two criminals, probably terrorists, one of whom heard him say 'Today you will be *with me* in Paradise' (Lk 23:43).

After he had risen from the dead and appeared to his disciples, they were convinced he was still with them in an even more intimate way than he had been before. They knew this when his Spirit dwelling in them transformed them from the frightened men who deserted him, ran away and, in the case of Peter, denied him, into fearless heralds of his resurrection before the very people who had had him crucified.

It was not only those who had known Jesus in the days of his flesh who were conscious of intimacy with him through the Spirit. All who believed in him, and were baptised into the company of his followers, shared communion with him. They were taught Jesus' words 'Where two or three are gathered in my name, there am I in the midst of them' (Mt 18:20) by those who had heard him speak. They met on the first day of the week, the day of his resurrection, to break bread together, and knew that they were taking part in the communion of his body and blood.

St Matthew quotes the Emmanuel text in the first chapter of his gospel, and he ends it with the promise of the risen Christ to his disciples: 'Lo, I am with you always, to the close of the age' (28:20). When Jesus ascended into heaven he did not cease to be man; he wears our nature at the right hand of God. No longer with us as he was historically in the first century AD, the incarnate Jesus is still with us according to his promise and through his Spirit. His presence with us in this age is a foretaste of the unimaginable glory of his presence at his final appearance. But though the nature of that manifestation is beyond our understanding, we can be sure that it will be the presence of the one who has united our humanity to his divine being. The seer of Patmos had a vision of a new heaven and a new earth when this age had come to an end, and heard a voice say 'Behold the dwelling of God is with men. He will dwell with them and they shall be his people, and God himself will be with them' (Rev 21:3). He uses the words 'dwelling' (*skéné*, literally 'tent') and 'dwell' (*skénósei*), which recall the fourth gospel's statement of the incarnation 'And the Word became flesh, and dwelt (*eskénósen*) among us' (Jn 1:14). The title 'Emmanuel' assures us that the God, who became man in Jesus, is with us in every age and for ever.

The antiphon continues by describing Emmanuel as 'the Desire of all nations, and their Salvation'. This is not the best translation of *Expectatio gentium et Salvator earum*, literally 'the expectation of the nations and their Saviour'. 'Expectation' repeats in a strengthened form the desire referred to in 'O King of the nations'. The phrase is not an exact quotation from Scripture but the idea is very common (eg. Ps 145:19).

Perhaps the verse which comes closest to it is 'For the creation waits with eager longing for the revealing of the sons of God' (Rom 8:19). The Greek word for 'eager longing' which the Vulgate translates *Expectatio*, literally means a waiting with head outstretched. The picture which it brings to mind is of someone on the lookout for an eagerly awaited visitor, neck craned, eyes fixed on the horizon for the first sign of his coming. Not only the nations but the whole creation, St Paul says, waits on tip toe for the final manifestation of God's glory, which includes human participation in that glory, 'the revealing of the sons of God.'

The repeated 'O ... come' in all the antiphons articulates this longing. When we pray these words in Advent, we both align ourselves with God's ancient people the Jews in waiting for the Messiah, and we also stretch forward in hope to the coming in glory of

Emmanuel who is now with us through His Spirit as a pledge and foretaste of that final, indescribable presence. There is no need in our prayer to distinguish these two comings. Together they form the longing of the human heart for God which runs through the Bible.

Humanity's longing for communion with God is not something confined to the chosen people or found solely in the Jewish scriptures. Traces of the search for the God who did not leave himself without witness in any nation (Acts 14:16,17) are found in the world's religions, philosophy and literature. In many and various forms, the hunger for Emmanuel, God among us, finds expression. Hindus believe in a number of incarnations (*avatars*), as Krishna explains to Arjuna, 'whensoever, O descendent of Bharata! piety languishes, and impiety is in the ascendent, I create myself. I am born age after age, for the protection of the good, for the destruction of evil-doers, and the establishment of piety' (*Bhagavad Gita*, ch. IV). While there is a great difference between the repeated incarnations of Hinduism and the unique incarnation of Christ, yet we can see in the words of the *Bhagavad Gita* a hint of the truth contained in the title 'Emmanuel'.

Similarly, the Roman poet Virgil, close to the time of Christ's birth, wrote in his fourth Eclogue of a 'golden age' about to dawn connected with the birth of a child. Some of the Church Fathers saw Virgil's words, rather fancifully, as an unconscious prophecy of Christ. At least we can say that the poet gave us language in which we can celebrate Christ's coming, as in the popular Christmas hymn, 'It came upon a midnight clear', which contains the line 'comes round the age of gold'. The yearnings of the human race find their answer in Emmanuel, God with us.

The one whom we await with eager longing is our Saviour (*Salvator*) and we pray to him 'Come and save us'. Emmanuel's name is Jesus, which means Saviour. The idea of 'God with us', as we saw, most often relates to his presence to deliver us from some danger or predicament. In our need of him, our alienation from the source of life and our captivity to the power of sin and temptation, God comes to us, becomes one of us, shares our condition of lostness and rescues us. It is God himself who is with us in our need and God himself who is our Saviour. The antiphon's reference to 'Saviour' and 'save', highlight the words in the Magnificat where Mary describes God as her Saviour and joyfully proclaims 'He has come to the help of his servant Israel'. We give a divine title to Jesus as we pray 'Come and save us, O Lord our God', echoing the words of doubting Thomas when he finally comes to faith and gives the clearest statement of Christ's divinity found in the New Testament (Jn 20:28). Jesus Christ is not simply God and man, but God precisely in the life and experience of a truly human being, who is in every respect one of us, except without sin. The climax of the antiphons is the proclamation of this great truth in the form of a prayer springing from the deepest human desire, to be reunited as forgiven sinners with him who made us and saved us.

O come, Emmanuel.

APPENDIX 1

The Latin text of the antiphons is that found in the *Breviarium Romanum*, 1870 edition.

O Sapientia, quae ex ore Altissimi prodiisti, attingens a fine usque ad finem fortiter, suaviterque disponens omnia: veni ad docendum nos viam prudentiae.

O Adonai, et dux domus Israel, qui Moysi in igne flammae rubi apparuisti, et ei in Sina legem dedisti: veni ad redimendum nos in brachio extento.

O Radix Jesse, qui stas in signum populorum, super quem continebunt reges os suum, quem gentes deprecabuntur; veni ad liberandum nos, iam noli tardere.

O Clavis David, et sceptrum domus Israel: qui aperis, et nemo claudit; claudis, et nemo aperit: veni et educ vinctum de domo carceris, sedentem in tenebris, et umbra mortis.

O Oriens, splendor lucis aeternae, et sol justitiae: veni, et illumina sedentis in tenebris, et umbra mortis.

O Rex gentium, et desideratus earum, lapisque angularis, qui facis utraque unum: veni, et salva hominem, quem de limo formasti.

O Emmanuel, Rex et legifer noster, expectatio gentium, et Salvator earum: veni ad salvandum nos, Domine Deus noster.

APPENDIX 2

The text of the Latin hymn is that given in *A Historical Companion to Hymns Ancient and Modern*, edited by R.M. Moorsom, 1889.

Veni, Veni, Emmanuel!
Captivum solve Israel!
Qui gemit in exilio,
Privatus Dei filio,

Gaude! Gaude! Emmanuel
Nascetur pro te, Israel!

Veni, O Jesse virgula!
Ex hostis Tuos ungula,
De specu Tuos Tartari
Educ, et antro barathri.

Veni, Veni, O Oriens!
Solare nos adveniens,
Noctis depelle nebulas,
Dirasque noctis tenebras.

Veni, Clavis Davidica!
Regna reclude coelica,
Fac iter tutum superum,
Et claude vias inferum.

Veni, Veni, Adonai!
Qui populo in Sinai
Legem dedisti vertice
In majestate gloriae.